Physics Without Prior Knowledge

Become an Einstein in 7 days

Benjamin Spahic

Physics Without Prior Knowledge" is the English translation of the German
book "Physik ohne Vorkenntnisse". Some passages in the book therefore focus
on the European region. This does not have an impact on the content, the
modes of action and general understanding.

About the author

Benjamin Spahic M.Eng was born in Germany in 1995 and grew up in a village
with 8,000 inhabitants near Karlsruhe. His passion for technology is reflected in
his studies as an electrical engineer with a focus on information technology at
the University of Applied Sciences in Karlsruhe.

He then deepened his knowledge in the field of regenerative energy production
at the Karlsruhe University of Applied Sciences.

PBD  Verlag

Imprint:
Author: Benjamin Spahic
Address:
Benjamin Spahic
Konradin-Kreutzer-Str. 12
76684 Östringen, Germany
Editor/ Proofreading: Mentorium GmbH
Cover: Kim Nusko
ISBN Paperback: 9798482385371
Email: Benjamin-Spahic@web.de
Facebook: Benjamin Spahic
Physics without prior knowledge
First publication 31.09.2021
Distribution through kindledirectpublishing
Amazon Media EU S.à r.l., 5 Rue Plaetis, L-2338, Luxembourg

Content

1. Foreword

Physics is discussed everywhere, whether on public television, at school and university or in private circles. But what is physics exactly? How can it be distinguished from mathematics and what do we need it for?

Physics describes a super-area of many sub-areas of the technical world. Velocities, electrical currents, mechanical forces or light rays and their refraction. All these areas are subsumed under the term physics. And that makes sense, because the description of all these natural laws can be calculated in the same way.

We encounter physics every day. Just think of all the achievements that have been made thanks to breakthroughs in physics. This doesn't necessarily just refer to major events like landing on the moon, but those that get us through life each day.

In the morning, we are woken up by our smartphone or digital alarm clock. The aerodynamics of our car, together with the physical calculation of acceleration and braking forces, get us to work safely and quickly. Almost every new type of technology is based on fundamental, physical planning and calculation.

Physics is important and unavoidable in many areas of life.

Despite its importance, however, there is one big problem: the enthusiasm for understanding and learning physics is very limited in society. Only a small, elite section of society studies the subject area.

Since you bought this book, it can be assumed that you are interested in the basics of physics. Maybe you are still a pupil who is considering studying physics, maybe you are an industrial engineering student who wishes to catch up, or maybe you are a retiree who finally wants to catch up on what is not taught well enough at school and in your studies. In any case, you won't regret getting to grips with the subject matter.

When one deals with physics for the first time, one finds various books on the subject, some of which consist of over 500 pages. Of course, these books also have their raison d'être, for example if you want to scrutinise and understand the subject matter down to the smallest detail, but for the majority of those interested, this is neither necessary nor effective.

However, these books are completely unsuitable for newcomers. They contain pages of mathematical derivations that are forgotten after a week. As a result, confusion quickly spreads. This is demotivating and quickly leads to many people giving up on the subject and reinforces their belief that "physics is not for me".

This is not because of the readers, but because they simply do not belong to the book's target group. You don't have to be an Einstein to understand the basics, you just have to be motivated to deal with the subject matter, as Einstein himself already knew.

> *"I have no special talent, I am just passionately curious. "*

> *-Albert Einstein*

With the right guide and a dose of motivation, anyone can understand the basics in no time. It is precisely from this mindset that this book has emerged.

It is a beginner's guide for inquisitive people who want to learn the basics of physics without much prior knowledge.

Prerequisites and level of knowledge:

This book is suitable for anyone with a basic enthusiasm for technology and mathematics. The basic knowledge of mathematics, such as transforming equations or the relationships between sine and cosine, is important and is therefore repeated in the first chapters. The repetition only serves to refresh the level of knowledge. This is followed by an introduction to the basics of physics.

It is not assumed that one already knows physical units or formulas -- even if this will certainly be the case for one or the other. The focus is on understanding and applying the correct formulae - without prior knowledge. For this purpose, complex physical relationships such as derivatives and integral calculus are simplified.

For a better structure, the following symbols can be found throughout the book:

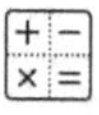 Arithmetic symbols: here the subject matter becomes more complex. A digression or derivation is given. The derivation of a topic is helpful for understanding, but it is not essential and is intended for reference.

 Light bulb: here the key points of a chapter are summarised. These statements are good for reference or when reviewing a topic area.

 Attention: common mistakes are mentioned here. It is shown where and why one often encounters obstacles or makes the wrong assumptions.

 Calculator: sample calculations or comprehension questions to follow up and help you to revise and take in the content.

Notation in this book:

Terms in bold: Terms that are to be newly introduced or particularly emphasised.

Italicised terms: Variable names, functions and other terms that are to be set aside from the continuous text.

Now I hope you enjoy reading and immersing yourself in physics!

1. Basics of mathematics

When you immerse yourself in physics, juggling terms and equations becomes the order of the day. Mathematics provides us with the basis for this. It serves as a tool.

Just as a carpenter needs to know how to use a hammer and chisel, we need to know how to properly summarise or simplify formulas. Basic arithmetic laws, function types and number systems are covered below. Those who have obtained a university entrance qualification will already know most of the areas, but partial aspects are also discussed that one only learns at technical high schools, for example.

Experience has shown that mathematics is a necessary evil, which is why each subject area is only dealt with as far as it is important for the understanding of this book. This includes first and foremost the conversion or solving of equations and the notation of powers.

1.1. Solving equations

The aim of solving an equation is to rearrange the equation so that we end up with the variable we are looking for on one side of the equals sign.

$$3x + 8 = -2x + 3$$
$$\dots$$
$$x = -1$$

To do this, we need to edit the equation in several steps to isolate the variable.

 When solving an equation, you transform it step by step until the variable you are looking for (e.g. x) is alone and positive on one side. The transformations are called **equivalent transformations**. This does not falsify the statement of the equation.

For example, we can add or subtract a constant or variable on both sides of an equation, or multiply, divide, increase, etc. both sides by a factor. When applying an equivalence transformation, write it at the end of the line together with a vertical line.

$$
\begin{aligned}
3x + 8 &= -2x + 3 &&\quad | + 2x \\
5x + 8 &= 3 &&\quad | - 8 \\
5x &= -5 &&\quad | : 5 \\
x &= -1
\end{aligned}
$$

All transformations must always take place on both sides of the equation. We will encounter the transformation of equations several times in each chapter.

1.2. Exponential functions

Exponential functions occur more often in everyday life than we assume. Almost every natural process can be traced back to an exponential function. This includes the growth of bacteria, the heating or cooling of any matter (whether food, sand or metal) or electrotechnical processes such as the charging and discharging of accumulators, battery storage or capacitors. In order to understand how these processes work, we must first turn to the mathematical basics - the exponential functions.

An exponential function is a function of the form

$$f(x) = a^x.$$

Here, a is called the base and x the exponent (colloquially high number). The base must be a real number that is greater than 0 and not equal to 1. The exponent is usually part of the real numbers. Note also the case $x = 0$.

$$a^0 = 1$$

for any base a.

1.3. Power laws

Power laws are applicable to terms with similar properties and allow us to summarise powers more clearly. In electrical engineering, you have to calculate a lot with exponents, so it helps if you have a few tricks at hand.

   All the following equations always work in both directions!

Power with negative exponent

If the exponent of a power is negative, the power can be rewritten as

$$a^{-b} = \frac{1}{a^b}$$
$$2^{-2} = \frac{1}{2^2}$$

Multiplication of powers with the same base

If two or more powers with the same base are multiplied together, the exponents add up. The base remains unchanged.

$$a^b \cdot a^c = a^{b+c}$$
$$3^2 \cdot 3^5 = 3^{2+5} = 3^7$$

Division of powers with the same base

If two or more powers with the same base are divided, the exponents subtract. The base remains unchanged. The derivation is obtained by writing the division as multiplication with a negative exponent.

$$\frac{a^b}{a^c} = a^b \cdot a^{-c} = a^{b-c}$$

$$\frac{2^5}{2^3} = 2^{5-3} = 2^2$$

Multiplication of powers with equal exponents

If two or more powers with the same exponent but different bases are multiplied together, the bases are multiplied. The exponent remains unchanged.

$$a^c \cdot b^c = (a \cdot b)^c$$
$$2^5 \cdot 3^5 = (2 \cdot 3)^5 = 6^5$$

Division of powers with equal exponents

If two or more powers with the same exponent but different bases are divided, the bases are divided. The exponent remains unchanged.

$$\frac{a^c}{b^c} = \left(\frac{a}{b}\right)^c$$

$$\frac{2^5}{3^5} = \left(\frac{2}{3}\right)^5$$

Exponentiating powers

If a (base with) power is exponentiated, the exponents are multiplied together.

$$(a^b)^c = a^{b \cdot c}$$

$$(2^3)^5 = 2^{3 \cdot 5} = 2^{15}$$

1.4. Logarithms

Logarithms occur just as frequently as exponential functions in everyday life. For example, in the human ear, in natural decay, pH values or our perception of brightness.

The basic arithmetic operations, i.e. "plus and minus" as well as "times and divided" are well-known. For every mathematical operation there is a corresponding inverse function. For example, if you want to reverse an addition, you subtract; a multiplication is reversed by means of division. The logarithm function is used to reverse exponentiation.

For example, we are about to solve the equation: $10^x = 1000$

To obtain the solution, i.e. our searched variable x, we apply the logarithm function to the base 10, colloquially "we draw the logarithm to the base 10". The number in the logarithm is called the numerus or logarithmand.

$$log_{10}(10^x) = log_{10}(1000)$$

$$x = 3$$

The base is written as an index to the logarithm.

In other words, the logarithm solves the problem: "To what number do I have to take the base (10 in the example) to get the result (1000)". The answer in the example is three, because

$$10^3 = 1000$$

For each base there is a corresponding logarithm. Some occur more frequently and have therefore been given their own abbreviation.

Logarithms table

The following table shows the notation of the logarithms to the base

Base of the logarithm	Notation	Designation
Any number a	$log_a z$	Logarithm to base a
2	$ld\ z = log_2 z$	Logarithm of two (Logarithmus dualis)
e	$ln\ z = log_e z$	Natural logarithm
10	$lg\ z = log_{10}$	Logarithm of ten

The **natural logarithm** is the logarithm most commonly used in mathematics. The logarithm of two is often used in the IT sector, as a computer works digitally, i.e. calculates in a binary way using only ones and zeros.

1.5. The Greek alphabet

In addition to solving equations and the power laws, we often use the Greek alphabet in physics, using both upper and lower case letters. The names will be repeated in the coming chapters. The Greek alphabet has a similar structure to ours and is therefore easy to understand. We do not have to learn the complete alphabet by heart. The letters we need will be explained in more detail in the coming chapters. Nevertheless, an overview and a reference page is useful when we are looking for the pronunciation or a certain letter.

The following table shows the Greek alphabet, in both upper and lower case.

Capital letter	Lower case	Pronunciation
A	α	Alpha
B	β	Beta
Γ	γ	Gamma
Δ	δ	Delta
E	ε / ϵ	Epsilon
Z	ζ	Zeta
H	η	Eta
Θ	θ ϑ	Theta
I	ι	Iota
K	κ	Kappa
Λ	λ	Lambda
M	μ	My [mü]
N	ν	Ny [nü]
Ξ	ξ	Xi
O	ο	Omicron
Π	π	Pi
P	ρ	Rho
Σ	σ	Sigma
T	τ	Tau
Y	υ	Ypsilon
Φ	φ / φ	Phi
X	χ	Chi
Ψ	ψ	Psi
Ω	ω	Omega

1.6. Sine, cosine, tangent

In addition to applying arithmetic laws, we will look at some trigonometry.

Sine, cosine and tangent describe the **ratio of the length of** two sides within a right triangle.

The triangle consists of two **cathets** and a **hypotenuse**. The cathetus which is adjacent to the angle α and the right angle is called the **adjacent side of α**. The side opposite the angle α **is** called the **opposite side cathetus.**

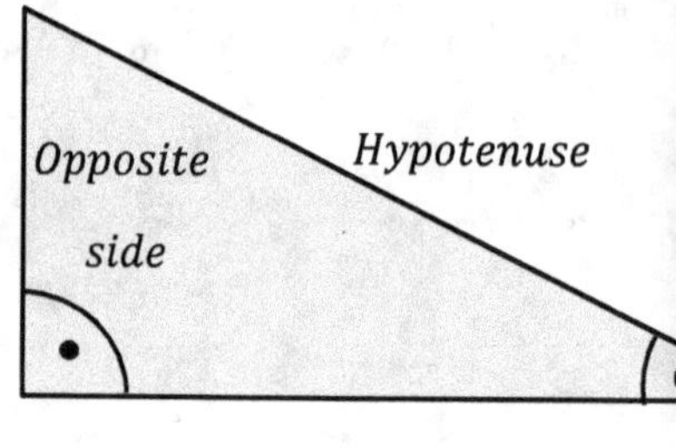

Figure 1: Right-angled triangle

$$\sin \alpha = \frac{\text{Opposite side}}{\text{Hypotenuse}} = \cos(\alpha - 90°)$$

$$\cos \alpha = \frac{\text{Adjacent side}}{\text{Hypotenuse}} = \sin(\alpha + 90°)$$

$$\tan \alpha = \frac{\sin \alpha}{\cos \alpha} = \frac{\text{Opposite side}}{\text{Adjacent side}}$$

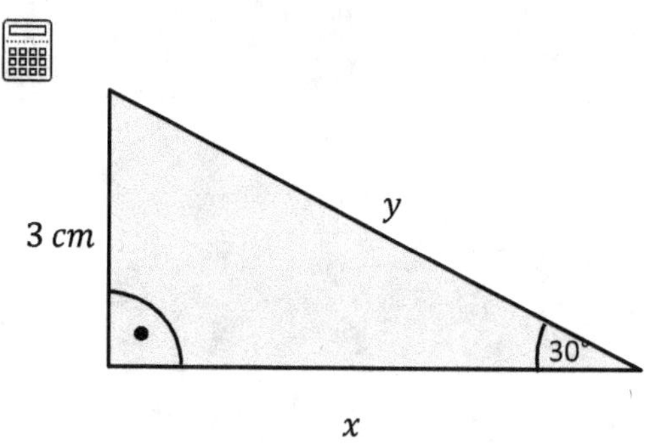

Figure 2: Sine and cosine on the right-angled triangle

$$\sin(30°) = \frac{\text{Opposite side}}{\text{Hypotenuse}} = \frac{3\ cm}{y}$$

$$\cos(30°) = \frac{\text{Adjacent side}}{\text{Hypotenuse}} = \frac{x}{y}$$

$$\tan(30°) = \frac{\sin \alpha}{\cos \alpha} = \frac{3\ cm}{x}$$

$$=> y = \frac{3\ cm}{\sin(30°)} = \frac{3\ cm}{0,5} = 6\ cm \qquad => x = \frac{3\ cm}{\tan(30°)} = \frac{3\ cm}{0,577} \approx 5,2\ cm$$

Basics of mathematics

1.7. Sine and cosine functions

If the hypotenuse is set to one in a triangle, the sine of an angle corresponds to its opposite cathetus, the cosine of the angle to its opposite cathetus.

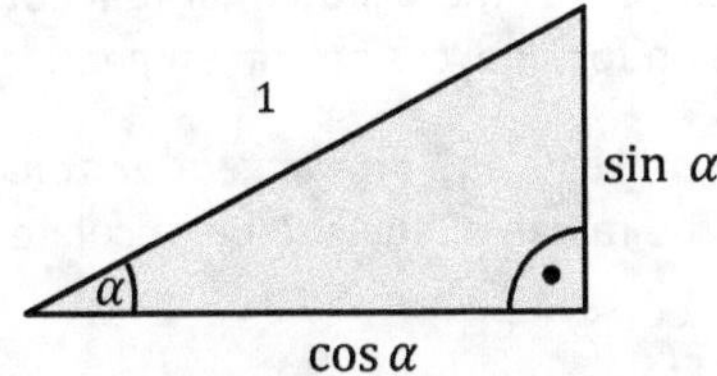

Figure 3: Sine and cosine for hypotenuse of length 1

$$\sin \alpha = \frac{\text{Opposite side}}{\text{Hypotenuse}} = \text{Opposite side} \quad ; \cos \alpha = \frac{\text{Adjacent side}}{\text{Hypotenuse}} = \text{Adjacent side}$$

If the angle α is then changed from 0° to 360°, we obtain a function that expresses the value of the opposite or adjacent side as a function of the angle.

Instead of specifying the angle in degrees, it is usual to use a conversion to circle angles or **radians**, the so-called **radians.** A circle with the radius $r = 1$ has a circumference of $U = 2\pi$. This circumference is used as a reference for a full angle of 360°. 360° corresponds to 2π. 180° corresponds to π and so on. The angle α becomes $x = \frac{\alpha}{360°} \cdot 2\pi$.

If we plot the length of the sine and cosine over the angle, we get the sine and cosine function respectively.

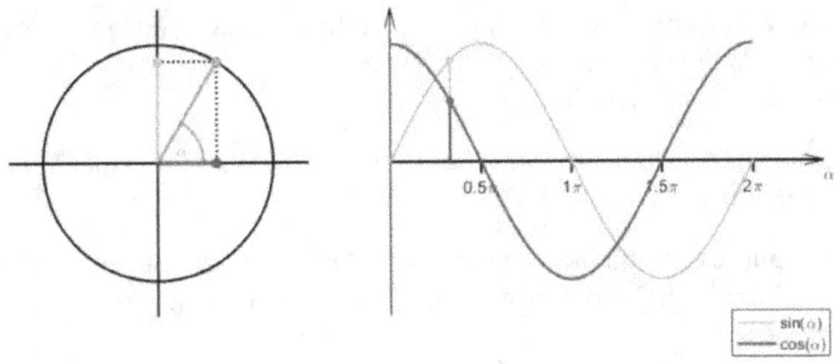

Figure 4: Sine and cosine function

Every natural oscillation consists of superimposed sine and cosine functions.

1.8. Arc sine, arc cosine, arc tangent

The sine, cosine and tangent functions map a ratio or a number onto an angle or a radian value. Just as the square root is the inverse function of exponentiation or the logarithm function is the inverse function of the expotential function, there is also the corresponding inverse function for sine, cosine and tangent.

The **Arcussinus** *arcsin*(), **arc cosine** *arccos*() and **arc tangent** *arctan*() are the inverse functions and allow the radian or angle to be calculated from the ratio value.

In the example $\sin \alpha = 0.5$ we apply the arc sine to compensate the sine function and get back the corresponding angle.

$$\sin \alpha = 0.5$$

$$\mathrm{arcsin}\,(\sin \alpha) = \mathrm{arcsin}\,(0.5)$$

$$\alpha = \mathrm{arcsin}(0.5) => \text{Calculator } \alpha = 30°$$

Often instead of $\mathrm{arcsin}(x)$ the expression $\sin^{-1}(x)$ is used. Analogously $\cos^{-1}(x)$ for the arc cosine or $\tan^{-1}(x)$. Strictly speaking, this is wrong, for example $\sin^{-1}(x) = \frac{1}{\sin(x)} \neq \mathrm{arcsin}\,(x)$.

This does **not** correspond to the arcussinus. However, the expressions $\sin^{-1}(x)$, $\cos^{-1}(x)$, and $\tan^{-1}(x)$ are widely used and anyone familiar with the subject knows that the arc functions are meant.

1.9. Two-dimensional coordinate system

Before we can conclude the chapter on mathematics, we will look at the representation of numbers and functions in coordinate systems. We will use the **Cartesian coordinate system**.

Most people remember this from school. Cartesian means that the axes are perpendicular to each other.

For the purposes of this book, we will limit ourselves to two dimensions with two axes. The horizontal axis is called the abscissa axis and is more simply referred to as the x-axis.

The vertical axis, on the other hand, is called the ordinate axis, the vertical axis or simply the y-axis. We will not consider the spatial depth, which is a third dimension, otherwise it can quickly become complex. The calculations are analogous for two coordinate axes.

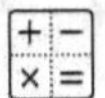

We can enter points in this coordinate system. A point in the mathematical sense is a circle with an infinitely small radius. A point is usually represented as a cross, rectangle or circle. A point has an **x** and a **y coordinate.**

P = (x|y)

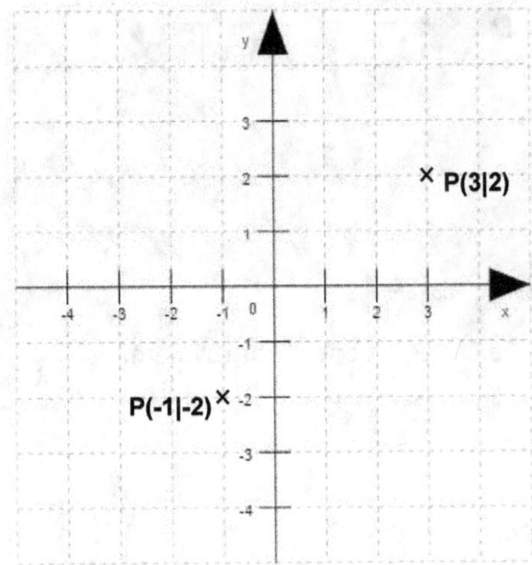

Figure 5: Cartesian coordinate system

 It is important to understand that a coordinate system always refers to an **origin** or the **zero point,** which we can determine ourselves!

This always has the coordinates **(0|0).** The zero point can be the corner of a room, the starting point of a racetrack or, as on the world map, our poles. Most of the time it results from a task.

 By cleverly choosing the zero point, subsequent calculations can often be simplified.

The great advantage of coordinate systems is that we can represent mathematical facts graphically. This gives us a clearer picture and facilitates understanding.

In addition to individual points, we can also graphically represent entire functions in a coordinate system.

The function assigns a y-value to each x-value. For an infinite number of values, this results in a continuous line, the graph of the function.

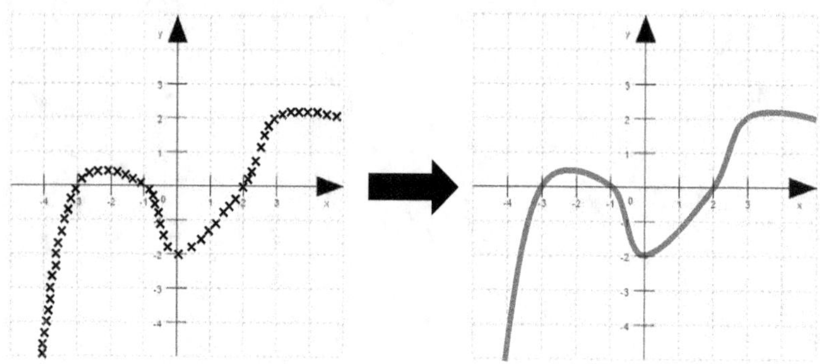

Figure 6: Points in the coordinate system become the function graph

This concludes our brief review of the Cartesian coordinate system.

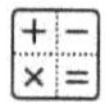

There are many more coordinate systems than you might think. For example, the position of a point (in relation to the origin) can be described not only as length (x-axis) and height (y-axis), but also as a radius from the origin and an angle. However, these are not relevant for this book and will therefore not be discussed further.

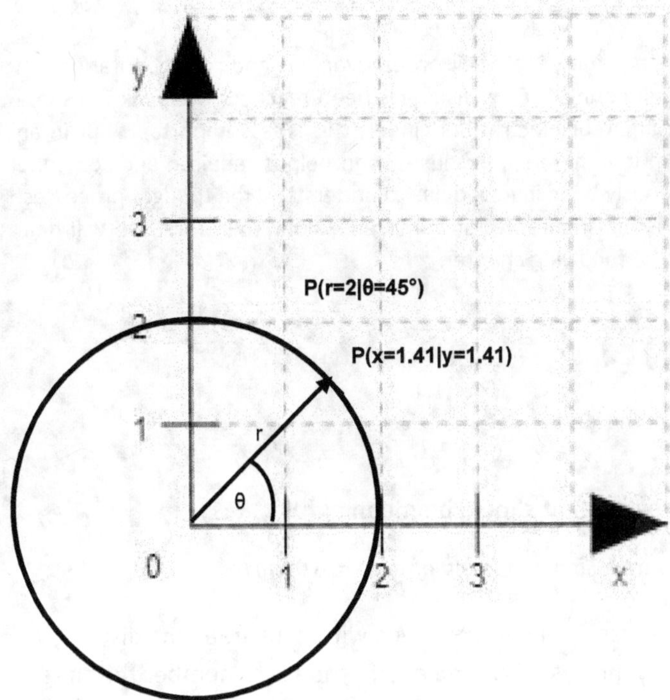

Figure 7: Illustration of two coordinate systems

2. Conventions in physics

After we have struggled through the mathematical basics, we can take care of some conventions in physics.

German engineers are known for their order, overview and correct notations. In many areas of engineering, a consensus has been reached to "speak the same language". As an amateur electrical engineer, this is less important, but in an international team it is more so. Because when help is required and someone who has not previously been involved has to understand the thought processes, correct notation is indispensable for comprehension. Therefore, we will deal with this topic in the following chapter.

2.1. Notation, upper case letters, lower case letters

The most important notation rules are:

1. If an index is set, it should be meaningful.

   The car is travelling at a speed of $v_{car} = 10\ km/h$.

2. If there are several identical sizes within an area, one distinguishes by indices. The simplest method is to number the sizes consecutively.

   Car 1 drives along $v_1 = 10\frac{km}{h}$, car 2 drives along $v_2 = 20\frac{km}{h}$.

3. There is no rule on how to assign indices. However, it has become accepted that an initial value is given the index zero and then numbered consecutively.

   The car drives constantly with an initial speed of $V_0 = 10\frac{km}{h}$, then it accelerates with $5\ \frac{m}{s^2}$.

4. If a variable is time-dependent, we use lower case letters. In addition, the variable on which the size is dependent is indicated in round brackets.

The speed v of the car over time t is described by $v(t)$ described by

5. For digital content, such as this book, the convention is that there is a space between the number and the unit.

> The exception is the degree sign when we speak of an angle, but not when we speak of temperatures.

20 °C, but an angle of 180°.

6. For physical quantities, the internationally common formula symbols are used.

$$R = U \cdot I$$

By adhering to these conventions, knowledge exchange is ensured evenly across national borders. Therefore in this book, as in every other textbook, we strictly adhere to the correct notation.

2.2. Prefixes for a wide dynamic range

Physics uses mathematics as a tool to put events into numbers and to be able to calculate with them. Since the world covers a very large range of values, **prefixes** were introduced. Instead of 1000 metres, one writes 1km, instead of 0.001 metres, one writes 1mm and so on. The following table shows an overview of the prefixes.

Designation	Decimal number	Power notation	Name	Abbreviation
One billiard part	0.000000000000001	10^{-15}	femto	f
One trillionth	0.000000000001	10^{-12}	pico	p
One billionth	0.000000001	10^{-9}	nano	n
One millionth	0.000001	10^{-6}	micro	µ
One thousandth	0.001	10^{-3}	milli	m
One	1	10^{0}	-	-
One thousand	1,000	10^{3}	kilo	k

One million	1,000,000		10^6	mega	M
One billion	1,000,000,000		10^9	giga	G
One trillion	1,000,000,000,000		10^{12}	tera	T
One quadrillion	1,000,000,000,000,000		10^{15}	peta	P

We recall the mathematical basics. We can always write prefixes as powers and then apply the power laws.

Let's take an example in which we are to calculate three km (kilometres) times five mm (millimetres). First, we write both values as a superscript.

$$3 \text{ km} = 3{,}000 \text{ m} = 3 \cdot 10^3 \, m$$

$$5 \text{ mm} = 0.005 \text{ m} = 5 \cdot 10^{-3} \, m$$

$$3 \text{ km} \cdot 5 \text{ mm} = 3 \cdot 10^3 \, m \cdot 5 \cdot 10^{-3} \, m$$

The base 10 is the same, therefore the exponents can be offset. The numbers before the exponents are calculated separately.

$$3 \cdot 10^3 \, m \cdot 5 \cdot 10^{-3} \, m = 3 \cdot 5 \cdot 10^3 \cdot 10^{-3} m \cdot m = 15 \cdot 10^{3-3} \, m^2 = 15 m^2$$

When invoicing, we split the numbers and their prefixes and charge them separately.

Calculate and simplify:
1. Three million times one billionth

2. Seven trillion times 4 thousandths

With units:
3. Five kilometres by 8 micrometres

4. One terranewton times 7 picometres

Solutions

$$3 \cdot 10^6 \cdot 1 \cdot 10^{-9} = 3 \cdot 10^{-3} = 0.003$$

$$7 \cdot 10^{12} \cdot 4 \cdot 10^{-3} = 28 \cdot 10^9 = 28{,}000{,}000{,}000$$

$$5 \cdot 10^3 \, m \cdot 8 \cdot 10^{-6} \, m = 40 \cdot 10^{-3} \, m^2$$

$$= 0.000004 \, m^2 \quad 1 \cdot 10^{12} \, W \cdot 7 \cdot 10^{-12} \, m = 7 \cdot 10^0 \, N \cdot m = 7 \, Nm$$

Remark:

Newton is the unit of force, which we will discuss in more detail later.

2.3. The "Système International d'unités"

We have already covered the conventions in physics. Not only is the correct notation enormously important, but also the units with which we calculate, as the following example shows:

In 1999, the Mars probe "**Climate Orbiter**" was lost when it entered the Martian atmosphere. At first, engineers puzzled over what had gone wrong.

The denouement was not long in coming and amounted to a sad comedy. A NASA supplier used the **English/Imperial** system of units and calculated the distances needed to land on Mars in **inches and feet**. A second NASA control team adopted the values but calculated in **metres and centimetres**. The data was accordingly incorrect and the probe burned up in the atmosphere on its approach to Mars. This expensive example shows how important it is to use a **uniform system.** In order to be able to calculate physical quantities in a meaningful way, an internationally valid system of units must therefore be introduced.

In technology, it is the "**Système International d'unités**".

 In the "Système International d'unités", exactly seven **base units were** defined. The units of the quantities are therefore also called **SI units.**

The SI units were almost all defined by natural constants. Each base unit is defined by a base quantity, a formula symbol and a unit or unit symbol. In the course of this book, we will deal with all physical quantities and their SI units. The following table with all seven base units is recommended as an overview.

Physical value	Formula symbol	Unit	Unit symbol
Time	t	Second	s
Length	s/l	Metre	m
Mass	m	Kilogram	kg
Current	I	Amps	A
Temperature	T	Kelvin	K
Amount of substance	n	Mol	mol
Light intensity	I_V	Candela	cd

It should also be noted that there are "naturalised" units. For example, one thousand kilograms is called one ton = 1000 kg = 1 t.

For units of length and area, the prefix centimetre/centimetre (1 cm = 0.01m), decimetre (1dm = 0.1 m) and an ar (1a = 100 m²) are also often used.

2.4. Derived SI units

In physics, there are many other quantities, such as the area A, the force N or the voltage U. All other quantities can be derived from the SI quantities. One therefore speaks of derived **SI units.**

The area A is a derived SI unit

$$Area = \text{Length} \cdot \text{Length} \; ; \; m \cdot m = m^2$$

It is common to write a physical quantity in square brackets and then state the unit.

For the purposes of this book, this convention will be maintained; if something is in brackets, it is a unit.

For example: The unit of time is the **second** $[t] = s.$

2.5. Representing differences

If you want to represent the difference of a quantity in physics, a **delta Δ is** used for this. For the difference between two quantities of energy, for example, one writes: $E_2 - E_1 = \Delta E$.

The large delta describes a **difference.**

The differential

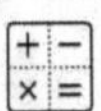 Let us now make this delta smaller and smaller in our thoughts. The values $E2$ and $E1$ continue to approach each other, but **never** become exactly the same. For this approximation of an infinitely small difference, one uses a **differential**. The large delta becomes a small d.

$$\Delta E \rightarrow dE$$

The change of one quantity after another is written as a differential. For example, speed is equal to the change in distance after time. As a differential representation:

$$v = \frac{s_2 - s_1}{t_2 - t_1} = \frac{\Delta s}{\Delta t} \rightarrow \frac{ds}{dt}$$

3. Movement and acceleration

In order to warm up to physics a little, let's get into a topic that still sounds very logical and intuitive to most people. Distances and speeds are something we can all imagine. Even terms like acceleration are familiar to every car driver who has ever pressed hard on the accelerator. But how can we calculate the correct physical quantities and what do we have to pay attention to? That's what we'll look at in this chapter. We will start with the first and simplest physical quantity.

3.1. The distance and displacement s

 The distance between two points A and B is called the **length** or **distance**. Its formula symbol is s or l and its SI unit is the **metre** $[d] = m$. Distances are often represented by arrows.

$$s = 5\,m$$

Figure 8: The route is shown as an arrow

We will explain later in the book why the representation as an arrow is not 100 % correct. A distance which represents a movement from A to B is called *displacement* instead.

In the context of this book, only the formula symbol s is used. s is often used in school lessons and in technical literature. In international works, the formula symbol l often appears in international works.

It is important to understand that a route needs a starting point (often also zero point) and an end point. **We determine** the start and end points and their designation **ourselves**. For the starting point, for example, we recommend the designation S_A (beginning) or S_0. The route is often abbreviated as the connection of the start and end points. $s = \overline{S_a S_b}$

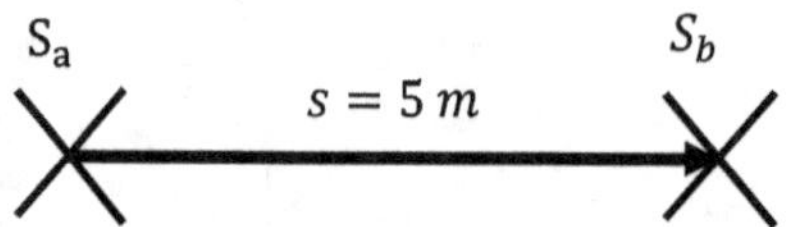

Figure 9: Route display with start and end point

We apply an imaginary scale to "measure" the distance. Depending on the inter-pretation, a point can also be negative.

Let's take a car as an example. We define the zero point at the beginning at the position where the car is. If the car drives 5m forward, it has covered a distance of $s = \overline{S_a S_{b2}} = 5\,m$. If, on the other hand, the car drives backwards, it has also covered a distance of $s = \overline{S_a S_{b1}} = 5\,m$ but it is now located at the point $S_{b2} = -5\,m$

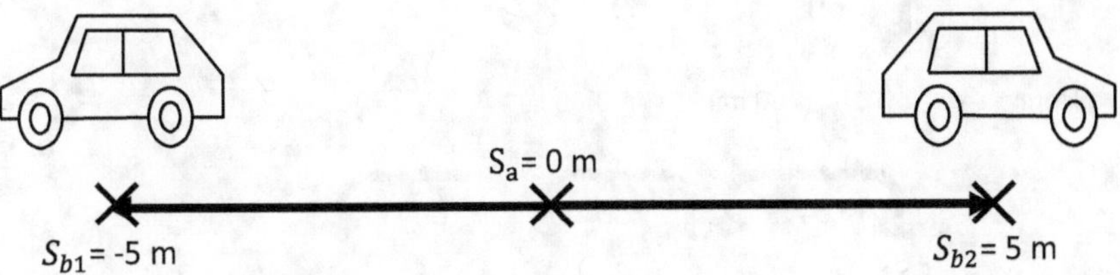

Figure 10: Negative location coordinates

The distance can be explained clearly. The next physical quantity we learn about is also known. It is **time**.

3.2. The time t

The physical quantity *time is* described by the formula symbol **t. The** unit of *time is* the **second** $[t] = s.$

Often in a task the time is not given in seconds, but in **minutes** (min), **hours** (h), **days** (d) or even **years** (a), then we must first calculate the time back to the basic unit of seconds.

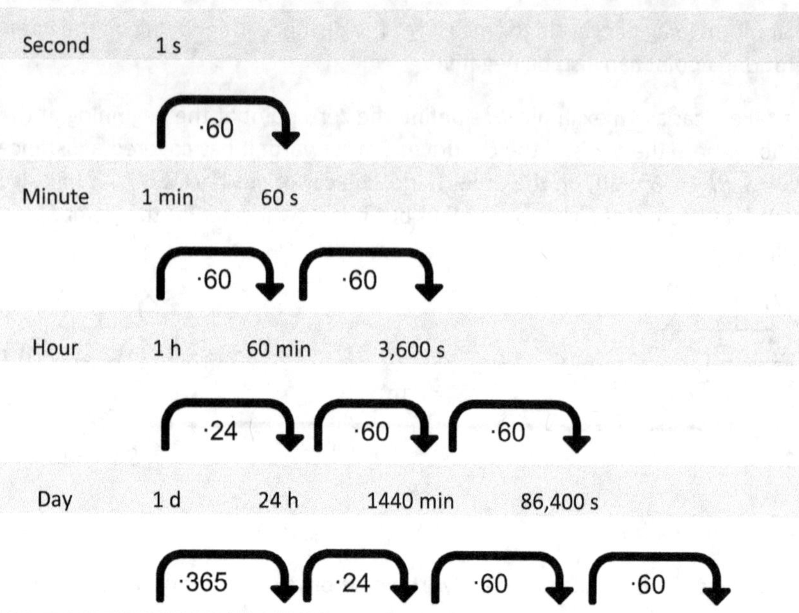

How many seconds are 21 minutes and 12 seconds?

How many seconds are there in 1 hour 34 minutes?

How many seconds are there in 1 day, 2 hours and 33 seconds?

$$21 \, min \cdot 60 \, \frac{s}{min} + 12 \, s = 1272 \, s$$

$$1 \, h \cdot 60 \, \frac{min}{h} \cdot 60 \, \frac{s}{min} + 34 \, min \cdot 60 \, \frac{s}{min} = 5640 \, s$$

$$1 \, d \cdot 24 \, \frac{h}{d} \cdot 60 \, \frac{min}{h} \cdot 60 \, \frac{s}{min} + 2 \, h \cdot 60 \, \frac{min}{h} \cdot 60 \, \frac{s}{min} + 33 \, s = 93.633 \, s$$

After getting to know the essential representation and interpretation of distances/displacement and briefly repeating the physical unit of *time*, we turn to the next physical quantity, the velocity v.

Movement and acceleration

3.3. The velocity v

 The **velocity** indicates the change in the distance over time and is abbreviated with the formula symbol v abbreviation.

$$v = \frac{s_2 - s_1}{t_2 - t_1} = \frac{\Delta s}{\Delta t}$$

The velocity consists of a direction and a magnitude (*speed*). Often the term *speed* is used when the direction of the velocity does not matter.

The unit of velocity v is accordingly $\frac{Meter}{Second}$; $[v] = \frac{m}{s}$

If we travel one metre in one second, we move with the speed $v = 1\,\frac{m}{s}$. If we travel 3 metres in half a second, we move with a speed of

$$v = \frac{3\ m}{0.5\ s} = 6\frac{m}{s}.$$

In physics we calculate with $\frac{m}{s}$. In everyday life the unit kilometre-per-hour is more common. $\frac{km}{h}$ is the common unit .

The units can be easily converted into each other.

One kilometre corresponds to 1000 metres. One hour corresponds to 3600 seconds. This results in

$$1\,\frac{m}{s} = \frac{\frac{1\ km}{1000\ m}}{\frac{1\ h}{3600\ s}} = 3.6\,\frac{km}{h} \quad \text{and analogue} \quad 1\,\frac{km}{h} = \frac{1000\ m}{3600\ s} = \frac{1}{3.6}\,\frac{m}{s} \approx 0.278\frac{m}{s}.$$

The conversion factor of $\frac{m}{s}$ in $\frac{km}{h}$ is **3.6**

or from $\frac{km}{h}$ in $\frac{m}{s}$ is $\frac{1}{3,6} \approx \mathbf{0.278}$

A pedestrian walks across a road that is 15 m wide at a traffic light within 10 seconds. What is the speed of the pedestrian in $\frac{m}{s}$ und in $\frac{km}{h}$?

Solution:

$$v = \frac{15\ m}{10\ s} = 1.5\,\frac{m}{s} = 1.5\,\frac{m}{s} \cdot 3.6\,\frac{km \cdot s}{m \cdot h} = 5.4\,\frac{km}{h}$$

A car is driving on the motorway at $120\,\frac{km}{h}$. How long does it take to travel 20 km? How many metres does it travel per second?

Solution:

We convert the formula $v = \frac{s}{t}$ *according to the variable t we are looking for.*

$$t = \frac{s}{v}$$

$$t = \frac{20\ km}{120\,\frac{km}{h}} = \frac{1}{6}h = 10\ min$$

Or in SI units:

$$20\ km = 20{,}000\ m\ ;\ 120\ km/h = 120\,\frac{km}{h} \cdot \frac{1}{3{,}6}\,\frac{h \cdot m}{km \cdot s} = 33.3\,\frac{m}{s}$$

$$t = \frac{20{,}000\ m}{33.3\,\frac{m}{s}} = 600\ s = 10\ min$$

The car travels 33.3 m in one second.

3.4. Uniform movements

We have already learned the basic equation for velocity.

$$v = \frac{s}{t}$$

In the derivation, we assumed a **constant speed**. Let's take our pedestrian from the above example, who crosses a road at a speed of $1.5\,\frac{m}{s}$ across a 15 m wide road. After one second the pedestrian has 1.5 m after one second, and after 2 seconds 3 m after 3 seconds 4.5 m and so on.

If we plot these pairs of values in a coordinate system where the X-axis represents time and the Y-axis represents distance travelled, we get the following graph:

Movement and acceleration

Distance in m

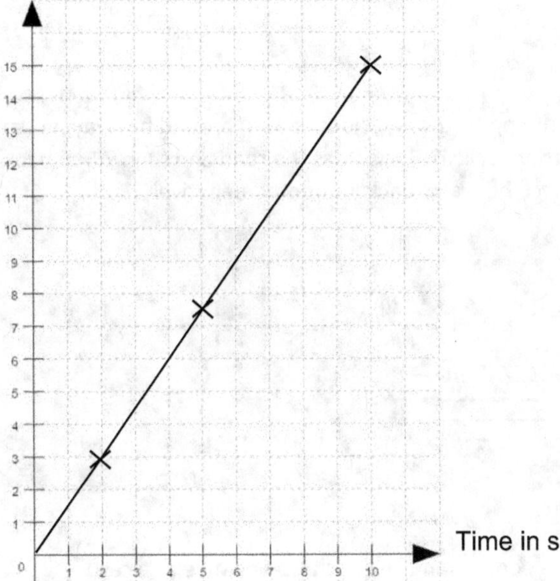

Figure 11: Linear time-distance diagram

The distance increases with time. What about the speed during this time? This is constant the whole time at $v = 1.5\ \frac{m}{s}$. If we enter this into the same coordinate system, we only get a constant.

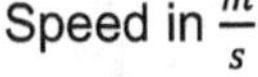

Speed in $\frac{m}{s}$

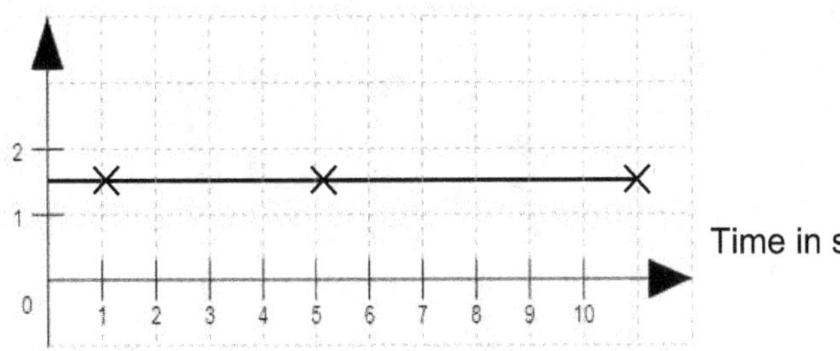

Figure 12: Constant time-velocity diagram

Movement and acceleration

3.5. Sectional, uniform movement

What happens if the pedestrian decides to turn around halfway, i.e. after 5 seconds? The pedestrian walks 7.5 m across the road and then 7.5 m back. Remember that the distance he walks back is counted negatively.

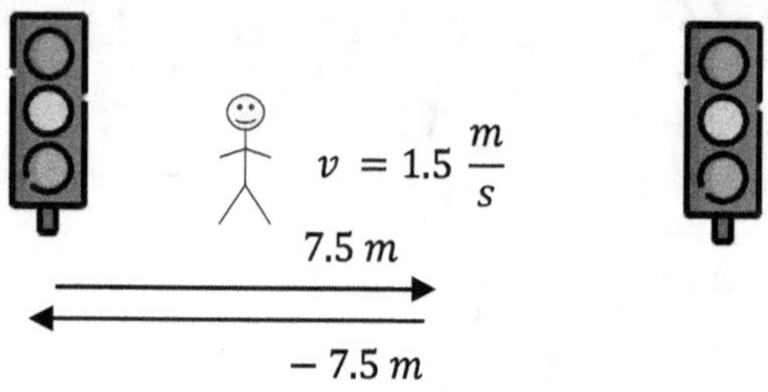

Figure 13: Reversing the speed at half distance

The speed that the pedestrian travels is also negative as a result.

$v = 1.5 \dfrac{m}{s}$ when running there

$v = -1.5 \dfrac{m}{s}$ when running back

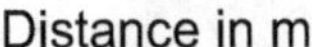

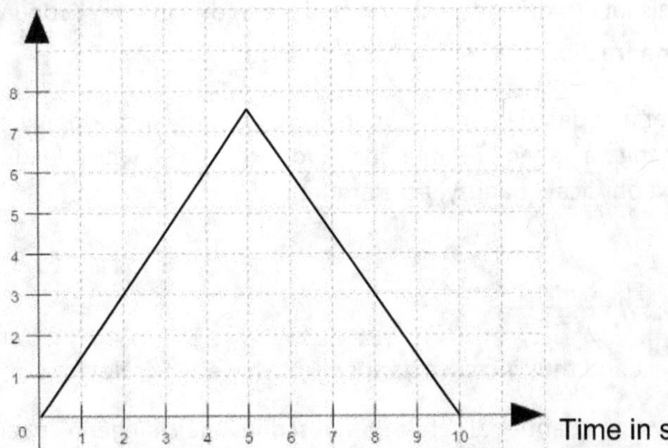

Figure 14: Time-distance diagram for reversal

The speed jumps from positive to negative when reversed.

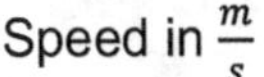

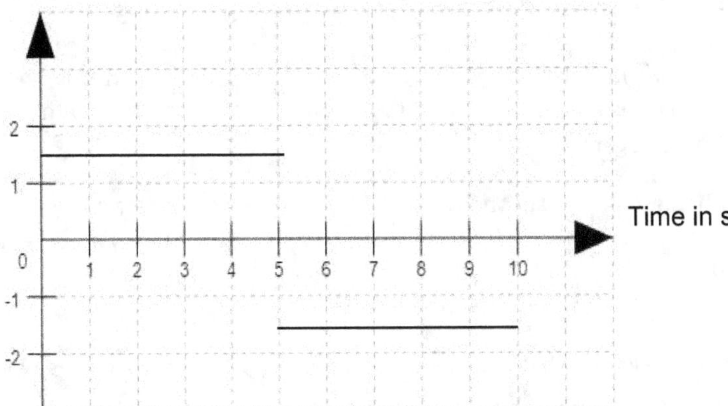

Figure 15: Time-velocity diagram for reversal

The velocities are constant in the individual sections, which is why we also speak of **sectional uniform motion**.

The table shows that the speed **jumps** at the rate of $t = 5\ s$ jumps.

If we transfer this fact to driving a car, it would mean that in one second we are $50\ \frac{km}{h}$ and after a fraction of a second $100\ \frac{km}{h}$ drive.

However, neither a pedestrian, a car nor any other object can suddenly change its speed. To change a speed, we must brake or accelerate, which leads us directly to the next physical quantity, acceleration.

3.6. The acceleration a

To move an object and thus increase its speed, we have to accelerate it.

The physical quantity **acceleration** describes the change in speed over time. Its formula symbol is a.

$$a = \frac{v_2 - v_1}{t_2 - t_1} = \frac{\Delta v}{\Delta t}$$

The unit of acceleration is accordingly $[a] = \frac{m}{s^2}$.

A metre-per-square-second is not a descriptive quantity. The unit results from the definition of acceleration as a change in velocity over time.

If we go from $0\ \frac{m}{s}$ to $1\ \frac{m}{s}$ this results in an acceleration of $1\ \frac{m}{s^2}$.

The term *braking* is also often used. Since we lose speed when braking, the speed before braking is greater than after ($v_2 < v_1$). Accordingly, Δv and thus the acceleration is negative.

If a car brakes in three seconds from $20\ \frac{m}{s}$ to $10\ \frac{m}{s}$ the acceleration is

$$a = \frac{10\ \frac{m}{s} - 20\ \frac{m}{s}}{3\ s} = -3.3\ \frac{m}{s^2}$$

If we want to know what speed we are travelling after a certain time, we rearrange the formula according to the speed.

$$a = \frac{v}{t} \rightarrow v = a \cdot t$$

When we accelerate $10\ s$ with $0.5\ \frac{m}{s^2}$ we get $5\ \frac{m}{s^2}$.

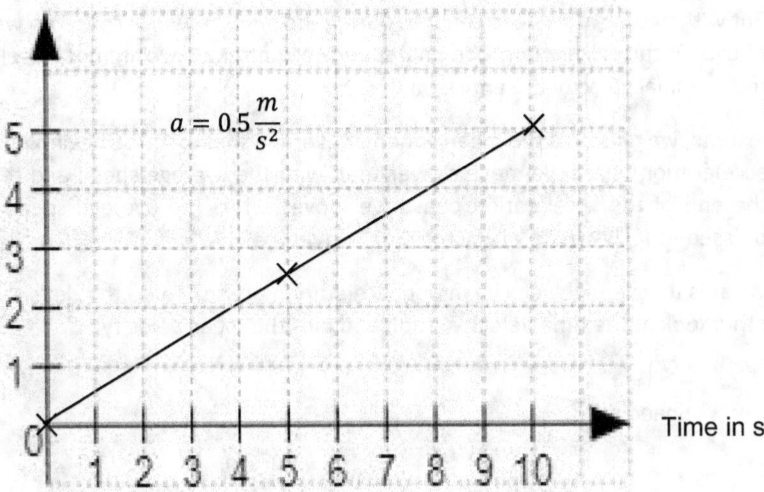

Figure 16: Linear time-velocity diagram during acceleration

A Tesla Model S accelerates from 0 to 100 in 2.5 seconds $\frac{km}{h}$. How great is the acceleration of the car?

$$100 \; \frac{km}{h} \cdot \frac{1}{3.6} \frac{m \cdot h}{s \cdot km} = 27.78 \; \frac{m}{s}$$

$$a = \frac{27.78 \; \frac{m}{s}}{2.5 \; s} = 11.1 \; \frac{m}{s^2}$$

A cycling professional accelerates with $2 \; \frac{m}{s^2}$. How fast is he after three seconds?

$$v = a \cdot t \rightarrow v = 2 \; \frac{m}{s^2} \cdot 3 \, s = 6 \; \frac{m}{s}$$

3.7. Uniformly accelerated movement

If we accelerate constantly, we speak of a **uniformly accelerated movement**. Compared to uniform motion, the speed changes depending on the acceleration.

We already know how to calculate the speed when we know the acceleration values. But what about the distance travelled? We remember that we calculate the distance of a uniform movement with $s = v \cdot t$.

But with people, the speed changes during the process, which speed do we have to use for the calculation? The final speed? No, after all, we are not travelling at the terminal velocity the entire time.

Instead, we must use the **mean speed** or **average speed.** At the beginning of the acceleration phase we move slower than with the average speed and towards the end of the acceleration phase we move faster. The average speed is expressed as $\bar{v}$ ("v-stroke", "v-across" or "v-average").

What is the average velocity in our acceleration phase? To do this, let's take another look at the time-velocity graph and plot the mean velocity.

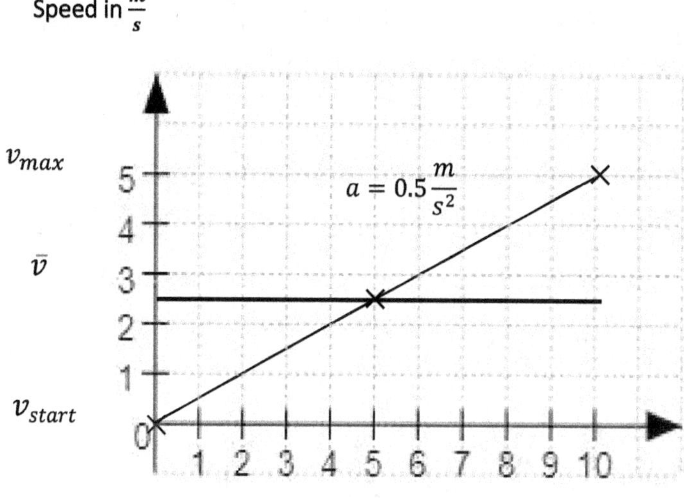

Figure 17: Average speed during acceleration

The average speed results from the average of the start and end speed. If the starting speed is zero, as in our case, it is calculated from $\bar{v} = \frac{1}{2} v_{max} = \frac{1}{2} a \cdot t$.

With the help of the average speed, we can finally calculate the distance travelled.

Movement and acceleration

$$s = \bar{v} \cdot t = \frac{1}{2} a \cdot t^2$$

So, we see that the distance is quadratically dependent on time. If we plot the distance on a graph, we get a parabola.

Distance in m

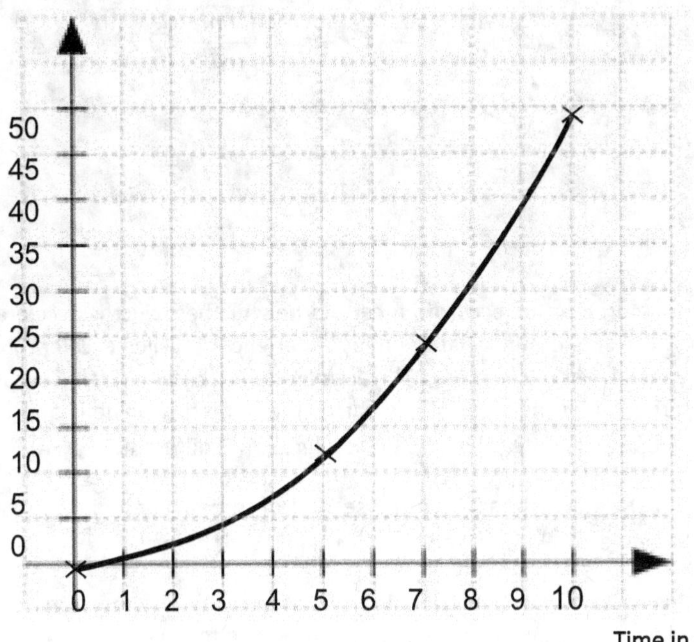

Figure 18: Square time-distance diagram

We have already calculated the acceleration of the Tesla Model S. With an average certification of $a = 11.1 \ \frac{m}{s^2}$ it needs 2.5 s from 0 to 100 $\frac{km}{h}$ to accelerate. What distance does the vehicle cover when accelerating?

We use two formulas that are available to us. Both lead to the same result.

$$s = \bar{v} \cdot t = \frac{1}{2} \cdot 27.78 \ \frac{m}{s} \cdot 2.5 \ s = 34.7 \ m$$

$$s = \frac{1}{2} a \cdot t^2 = \frac{1}{2} \cdot 11.1 \ \frac{m}{s^2} \cdot (2.5 \ s)^2 = 34.7 \ m$$

A car brakes with $a = 10\,\frac{m}{s^2}$ to $0\,\frac{km}{h}$. The braking distance is $50\,m$. How long did the braking process take and how fast was the car at the beginning of the braking process?

Solution:

$$s = \frac{1}{2}a \cdot t^2 \rightarrow 50\,m = \frac{1}{2} \cdot 10\,\frac{m}{s^2} \cdot t^2 \rightarrow t = \sqrt{\frac{50\,m}{10\,\frac{m}{s^2}}} = 2.23\,s$$

$$v = a \cdot t = 10\,\frac{m}{s^2} \cdot 2.23\,s = 22.3\,\frac{m}{s}$$

3.8. The free fall

When we drop an object from a certain height, the object is accelerated uniformly. The acceleration that the body experiences is called **acceleration due to gravity** and is abbreviated as **g**. The acceleration due to gravity is a constant that is determined by the mass of the earth. The numerical value is approximately $g = 9.81\,\frac{m}{s^2}$. On other planets, the acceleration is different.

 This means that after one second of free fall, an object already has a speed of $9.81\,\frac{m}{s}$. The mass is insignificant here.

A spring is accelerated just as fast as a stone. The difference in velocities is caused by air friction, not by the acceleration due to gravity.

Roller coasters often advertise with "g-forces". This describes the acceleration of the roller coaster compared to the acceleration due to gravity. The Silver Star roller coaster in the Europapark in Rust accelerates the passengers of the car with 4 g, four times the acceleration due to gravity, i.e. with just under $a = 39.24\,\frac{m}{s^2}$!

It must be said that this acceleration only affects the occupants for an extremely short time. After one second with an acceleration

Figure 19: Silver Star roller coaster

Movement and acceleration

of $39.24\frac{m}{s^2}$ the car would already be at $39.24\frac{m}{s}$ which is over $123\frac{km}{h}$.

The physical model of uniform motion or uniformly accelerated motion is simple and understandable. As is so often the case, the model can only be applied to reality to a limited extent; disturbance variables such as the friction of the tyres on the road or the air resistance force, which increases with speed, are not taken into account.

They ensure that the acceleration does not remain constant. For example, a car can accelerate from $0\frac{km}{h}$ $100\frac{km}{h}$ much faster than from $100\frac{km}{h}$ to $200\frac{km}{h}$.

In free fall too, there is a balance between air resistance and gravity, otherwise the speed would approach infinity over time.

 However, we can approximate the movements for **very small periods of time** very well with our physical models.

However, if the result deviates from our calculations, we must always keep in mind that complex disturbance variables are very likely to be to blame.

This concludes the first chapter of acceleration. The next chapter is really important because it is about forces!

4. Forces and mechanics

We encounter forces everywhere in everyday life. When carrying shopping bags, climbing stairs or doing leisure sports. Forces and their interactions are summarised in physics under the umbrella term 'mechanics'. Put simply, mechanics includes everything that moves and influences each other. In the 17th century, a well-known physicist named Isaac Newton established three important axioms that were named after him. An axiom is a principle or law. That is why Newton's axioms are also called Newton's laws or Newtonian principles. With the help of the axioms, predictions can be made.

Before we deal with the axioms, we ought to consider a few physical quantities that are important for understanding the axioms.

To make mechanics more tangible, we must first introduce a descriptive physical quantity, mass.

4.1. The mass m

Mass is a physical quantity, which is abbreviated with the formula symbol m. The SI unit is the **kilogram** $[m] = kg$.

The kilogram is a special SI unit. Contrary to what you might expect, the base unit is **not the** gram, but the kilogram, i.e. **1000 grams**. At first it is confusing that with every other unit you convert the prefixes, but not with the kilogram. The kilogram was not defined by natural constants, but by a reference stone. In France lies the **"original kilogram"**, which was used as a definition for 1kg.

If you don't have any background knowledge of physics, mass is often equated with the weight of a thing. Strictly speaking, this is not correct, but on earth it is true. The mass 1 kg also has a weight of one kilogram due to the Earth's gravitational pull. On the moon, on the other hand, there is only 0.165g, i.e. only 16.5% of the Earth's gravitational force. Accordingly, a mass of 1kg on the moon weighs only 165g. The mass has not changed. Nevertheless, one often speaks of *light* and *heavy* masses, although a small or large mass would be physically correct.

It gets more interesting when masses start to move, which leads us to the next physical quantity, momentum.

4.2. The momentum p

Momentum is a physical quantity that represents the product of the *mass* and *velocity* of a body. The impulse is abbreviated by the formula symbol p.

$$p = m \cdot v$$

The unit of the momentum is correspondingly $[p] = kg \cdot \frac{m}{s}$

Colloquially, momentum can be described as the "force" of a body. Momentum is decisive in the impact of one body on another.

We have all felt the force of a body at some point, for example when we have been hit by a football, tennis ball or golf ball. The damage caused by the ball depends on the weight of the ball and its speed. A table tennis ball, due to its low mass, causes much less damage when it hits us at the same speed than, for example, a bowling ball. The bowling ball has a much higher momentum.

Having learnt about momentum, we turn to Newton's first law.

4.3. Newton's 1st Law - The Principle of Inertia

The principle of inertia, also called the law of inertia or inertial law, states that every body maintains its speed and direction without external influence. A body that is at rest remains at rest. A body moving on a straight line will continue to move until it is deflected from its path by an external force.

In reality, a football will not fly straight for an infinite time. The gravitational force of the earth and the friction of the air have a constant influence on the ball. In space, on the other hand, things look different. Here, gravity and friction are almost non-existent. An object that we push in space will move straight ahead until it hits another object. In the process, the momentum is exchanged with the other object.

The principle of inertia states that the direction and amount of the momentum of a body can only be changed by an external force. Forces are the cause of a change in motion.

The principle of inertia is understandable, but it is a purely theoretical statement. We can say that the momentum of a body does not change without the application of force, but if we want to calculate with numbers, we need formulas. This is exactly what Newton described in his second law.

4.4. Newton's Second Law: The force F

Newton's second law is a consequence of the law of inertia.

To understand the implications, we must introduce a physical quantity whose unit was also named after the successful physicist.

The physical quantity **force** bears the formula symbol **F**. The unit of *force* is the **Newton** $[F] = N$.

The conclusion from Newton's 1st law is that we need a force to change the momentum in time. Expressed in formulas this means

$$F = \frac{\Delta p}{\Delta t}.$$

We also know that momentum is the product of mass and velocity.

$$p = m \cdot v$$

Since the mass does not change, a change in momentum can only change the velocity Δp.

$$\Delta p = m \cdot \Delta v$$

If we insert this relationship into the above formula for calculating the force, we get

$$F = \frac{\Delta p}{\Delta t} = \frac{m \cdot \Delta v}{\Delta t}.$$

Looking back over the last few chapters, can you recall whether we have seen the expression $\frac{\Delta v}{\Delta t}$ before? We have indeed, in the definition of acceleration!

$$a = \frac{v_2 - v_1}{t_2 - t_1} = \frac{\Delta v}{\Delta t}$$

If we put the acceleration into the previous formula, we get Newton's second law and one of the most important relationships in mechanics.

$$F = m \cdot a$$

 If a body is accelerated, the force acting on the body is directly proportional to its mass as well as to the acceleration.

The unit of mass is $[m] = kg$, the unit of acceleration is $[a] = \frac{m}{s^2}$

If a body with a mass of $m = 1\ kg$ is accelerated with an acceleration of $a = 1\ \frac{m}{s^2}$ the body is subjected to a force of $F = 1\ N$.

We also know this effect from driving a car. We experience a force when we step on the accelerator, but not when we drive constantly, because then the acceleration is zero.

The definition of the force gives the acceleration a a further meaning.

$a = \frac{F}{m}$. The unit of acceleration can therefore be expressed both as $\frac{m}{s^2}$ as well as $\frac{N}{kg}$ as the unit of acceleration. Both are correct. Depending on the task, the appropriate unit can be chosen.

On earth, every object is attracted with the acceleration due to gravity. The force exerted on a body is also called the weight force with the formula $F_g = m \cdot g$. Here, the difference between the weight or the weight force of a body and its mass becomes clear once again.

Therefore, in order to lift an object, we need a force that is greater than the weight force.

$$F > F_g = m \cdot g$$

What force acts on an occupant with a mass of $m = 80\ kg$ when accelerating in the Silver Star roller coaster ($a = 4\ g$; $g = 9.81\frac{m}{s^2}$)?

Solution:
$F = m \cdot a$

$$F = 80\ kg \cdot 4 \cdot 9.81\ \frac{m}{s^2} = 3139\ N = 3.14\ kN\ (Kilonewton)$$

A stone with the mass $4\ kg$ moves with $12\ \frac{m}{s}$. What is its momentum? What force acts on the stone? Hint: it is not accelerated.

Solution:

$$p = m \cdot v = 4\ kg \cdot 12\ \frac{m}{s} = 48\ \frac{kg \cdot m}{s}$$

Since the stone is not accelerated, no force acts on the stone.

To lift a crate of vegetables we need at least a force of $F = 120\ N$. How heavy is the crate?

Solution:

The acceleration that the box experiences is just the acceleration due to gravity. Therefore, the force we need to lift the box is just equal to the weight force

$F_g = 120\ N$. For the mass, this gives:

$$F_g = 120\ N = m \cdot 9.81\ \frac{m}{s^2}$$

$$m = \frac{120\ N}{9.81\ \frac{m}{s^2}} = 12.23\ kg$$

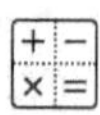

When determining the force, we assume that a change in momentum results from a change in velocity. The mass remains constant. However, the mass of a body can change.

These effects occur when, for example, a body moves at almost the speed of light. We are very far away from witnessing this in everyday life, which is why Newton's axioms can be applied.

Furthermore, a linguistic distinction is made between **classical mechanics/physics**, in which Newton's laws apply, and **modern physics**, which includes, for example, quantum mechanics and Einstein's theory of relativity.

4.5. Newton's 3rd Law - Reaction Principle

Newton's third law describes what happens when one body exerts a force on another body, the same force is simultaneously exerted by the second body on the first body. The direction of the forces is opposite, so that the sum is zero.

We can see this again in football, for example. When a player receives the ball with full force in the face, he sinks to the ground in pain. The ball has exerted a force on the player. In return, however, the player also exerts the same force on the ball.

Forces and mechanics

As a reaction, the ball does not stay at the feet of the player who has sunk to the ground, instead it bounces powerfully. Every action results in a reaction. This principle is also described as Actio = Reactio.

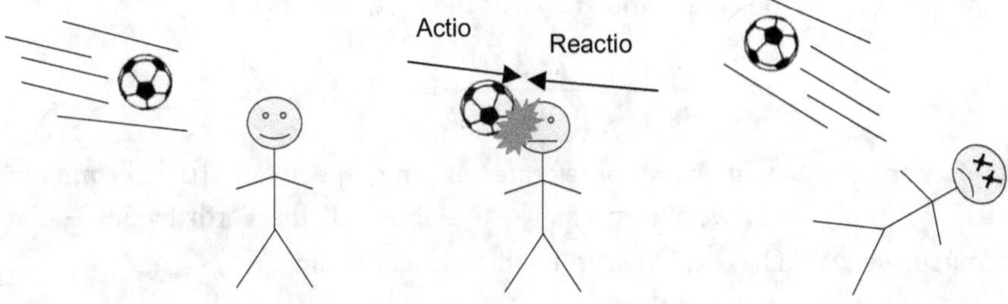

Figure 20: Actio = Reactio in a collision

Another example is starting a car. To accelerate a car, the wheel must exert a force on the road. According to Newton's third law, the road simultaneously exerts a force on the car. How can we imagine this? The car accelerates the earth by exerting a force on it? Sounds strange at first, that we are "pushing" the earth.

But that is indeed the case.

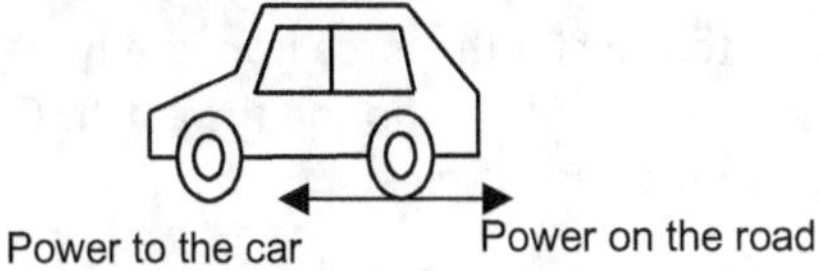

Figure 21: Force diagram during start-up

However, we also know that the acceleration $a = \frac{F}{m}$. The counterforce with which our car accelerates the earth is the same, but the earth has a mass of approx. $6 \cdot 10^{24}\ kg$ and our car has a mass of approximately $1000 - 2000\ kg$. So, the effect is negligible. Moreover, there are certainly other cars somewhere on the planet that accelerate in the opposite direction in the same second, so that the effect is cancelled out.

For fun, let's calculate the example anyway.

For this, we take our Tesla Model S again, which has an acceleration of $a = 11.1\ \frac{m}{s^2}$ has. The weight of the Tesla is just under $m = 2.1\ t$.

This means that our sports car exerts a force of $F = 2100\ kg \cdot 11.1\frac{m}{s^2} = 23.3\ kN$ on the road. The earth experiences a counterforce with the same value, but in the opposite direction.

This means that the acceleration towards the earth results in:

$$a = \frac{F}{m_{Erde}} = \frac{23.3\ kN}{6 \cdot 10^{24}\ kg} = 3.9 \cdot 10^{-21}\frac{m}{s^2}$$

This means that if we accelerate at the speed of $10^{21}\ seconds = 31.7\ billion\ years$, we would change the speed of the Earth by $3.9\ \frac{m}{s}$ - of course, we would have to drive at full throttle all the time.

Strictly speaking, we must bear in mind that the earth is not accelerating in a straight line, but is rotating. It is therefore a **rotation**. The analogous quantity of velocity for the rotational movement is the **angular velocity.** ω.

However, since the example is only a theoretical experiment that is not meant to be taken too seriously, we will not go into it further.

Back to reality. What happens if the road cannot apply the desired force, for example because there is not enough friction to transfer the force from the tyre to the asphalt? Then no force is exerted, neither on the tyre nor on the earth. The earth and the car do not accelerate because the wheel spins.

Another example of the third axiom is that the earth exerts a weight force on us and pulls us towards the centre of the earth. We have already learned about acceleration due to gravity g. However, a force counteracts the Earth's gravitational pull. Otherwise we would accelerate as if in free fall.

The force that counteracts the force of gravity is called the **normal force.** F_N is called normal force. The normal force can be thought of as the force that the ground exerts on us so that we are not accelerated into the ground. In free fall, the normal force is zero. When we are standing on the ground it is equal to the weight force. Finally, we are neither accelerated upwards nor downwards.

Forces and mechanics

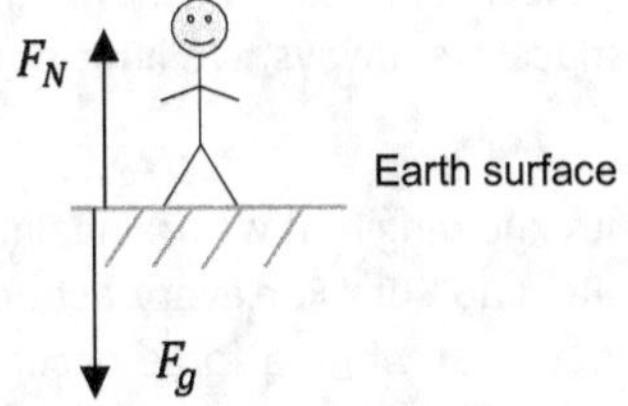

Figure 22: Force diagram normal force and gravity

We have already learned from the third axiom that forces not only have an amount (numerical value) but also **a direction.** We will learn how to represent forces in the following chapter.

4.6. Vectors and representation of forces

A **vector** is a mathematical entity represented by an arrow.

A vector has a *magnitude* (measurement), which is represented by the length of the arrow, and a direction. The opposite we have looked at so far is the **scalar.** A scalar has a magnitude but no direction.

Vectors are directional and location-independent, whereas a distance has a defined start and end point. So far, we have represented the distance as a vector (arrow), now we also understand the physical background.

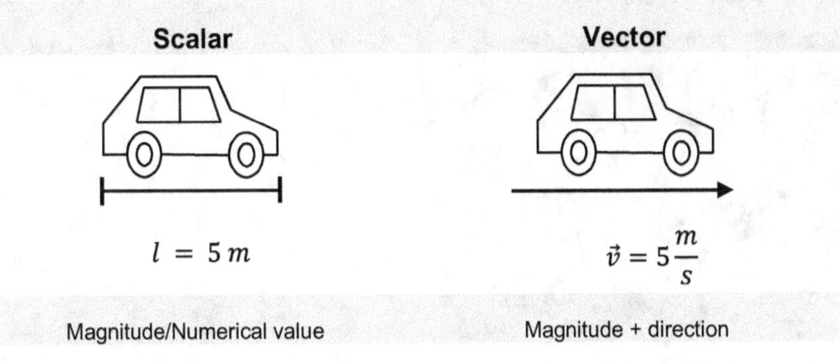

Once we know what a vector is, we can represent forces as vectors.

A force is given a magnitude. This value, as we have learned, is given in newtons. In addition, the force is assigned a direction in space. As always, we limit our-selves to a two-dimensional space.

Strictly speaking, we have already done this without knowing that we are dealing with vectors. The third Newtonian law "Actio = Reactio" or "**For** every action, there is an equal and opposite **reaction**." described that when a force occurs, there must always be an opposing force. For example, in our car.

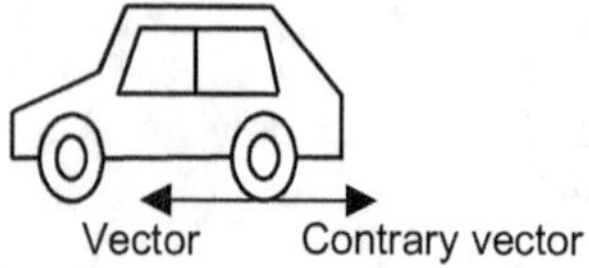

Figure 23: Vector representation Actio=Reactio

But what is the use of representing a force as a vector? Vectors have other prop-erties that are extremely helpful for calculating with forces or vectors. First of all, they can be added together.

4.7. Adding forces

There is not only one force acting on a body, but very often several. Each force has a different strength and different directions.

Let's take an example that some of you will certainly be familiar with. In classic tug-of-war, two teams with ten members each compete against each other and pull on two different ends of a rope.

Figure 24: Forces in different directions during tug of war

Now the question arises, in which direction does the centre of the rope move? In order to clarify this, we represent the forces that the teams exert on each other as vectors, so each force is understood as an arrow with length and direc-tion. All vectors start at the centre and point in the direction in which the rope is

Forces and mechanics

pulled. The length of the arrows indicate the strength of the force. Trained adults can apply a pulling force of up to 800 N. For a ten-man team, this is 8 kN. In the example, one team pulls with $F_1 = 8.5\ kN$ and the other only with $F_2 = 5.2\ kN$.

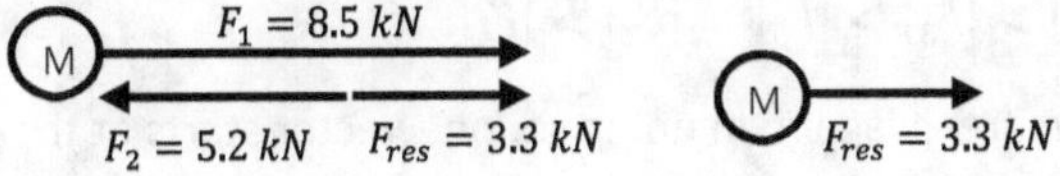

Figure 25: Force representation in tug-of-war

To obtain the resulting force, we take advantage of the fact that we can move the vectors freely. The force components that point directly in opposite directions neutralise each other. The creates a **resultant force (net force).**

Figure 26: Resultant force when forces are superimposed

As a result we get what was already obvious; the team that pulls more strongly on the rope moves the opposing team further and further towards it. The **centre M moves** in the direction of the stronger force. The resulting force is

$$F_{res} = F_1 - F_2 = 3.3\ kN$$

In this example, there are only two directions in which the rope can move. What happens if there are several forces acting in different directions?

As an example, let's imagine five ropes that are all knotted at one point, the centre point M.

At each of the five ends E1-E5, a person pulls in a different direction and with different forces. One person a little stronger, the other a little weaker.

To determine the resulting force, we again apply the representation as vectors.

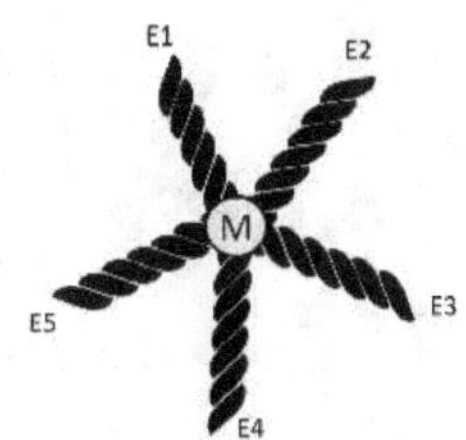

Figure 27: Various forces apply at the centre point M

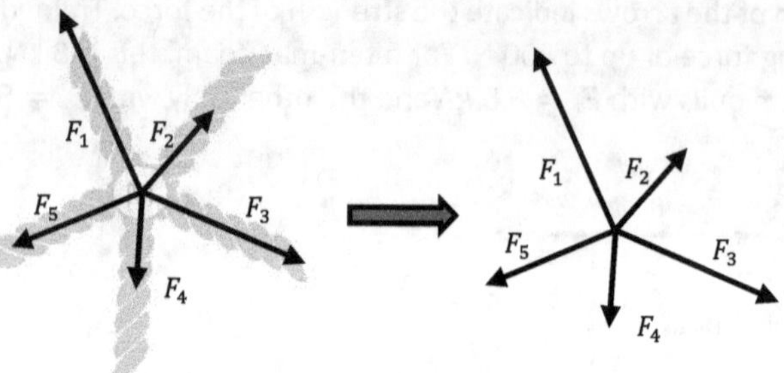

Figure 28: Representation as vectors

The length of the arrows again indicate the amount of the forces, i.e. the strength. In this example: $|F_1| > |F_3| > |F_5| > |F_2| > |F_4|$.

We can then move the vectors freely again. In doing so, one vector starts at the end of another. The order in which we move the vectors does not matter, the result is the same. For the example, we place the vectors next to each other according to the index.

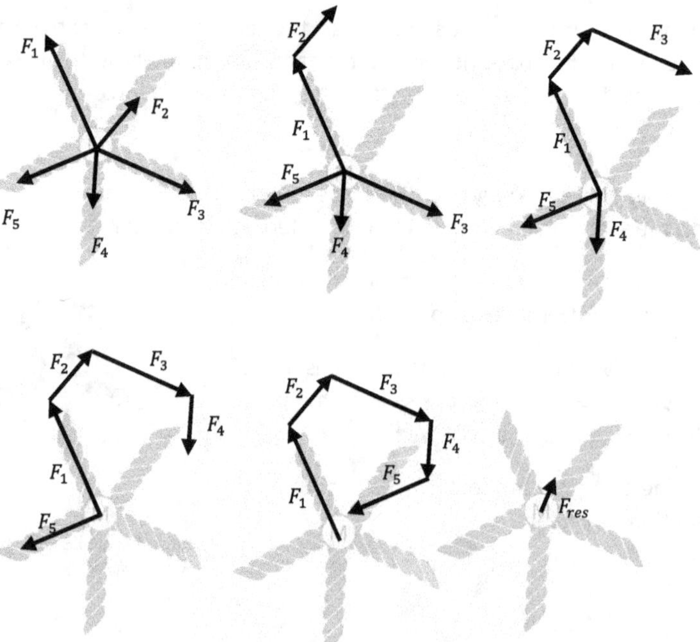

Figure 29: Graphical addition of forces

Forces and mechanics

We have determined the resulting force and its direction by adding up the individual forces. Formally we write for this $F_{res} = F_1 + F_2 + F_3 + F_4 + F_5 = \sum F$ (sum of all forces).

The amount of the resulting force corresponds to the length of the arrow.

Using the example, we also need to reconsider our formula for determining the force.

$$F = m \cdot a$$

In our example, F is the resulting force F_{res}.

This results in $F_{res} = m \cdot a$ respectively $\sum F = m \cdot a$

Without our vector theory, we would have been unable to determine either the direction or the magnitude of the resulting force.

The vector representation is still of great importance in the next chapter.

4.8. Forces in inclined planes

We already know how much force we have to use at least to overcome the gravitational force acting on a body with *mass m*, namely $F_g = m \cdot g$.

This relationship always applies when we lift an object directly against gravity. But what about when we carry the object up a hill? For example, when a car rolls down a hill. Is it then also accelerated with the $g = 9.81 \, \frac{m}{s^2}$ acceleration? Let's take a closer look at the situation and consider which forces are responsible for the acceleration.

The weight force always acts perpendicular to the ground. We call the accelerating force the downward **slope force** and it acts along the inclined plane.

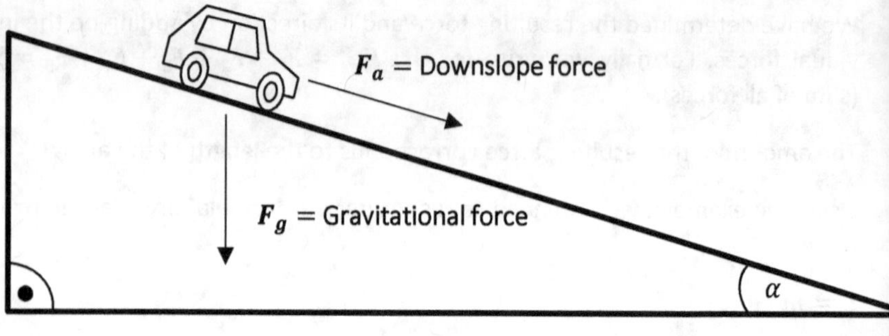

Figure 30: Slope down force on a sliding plane

It becomes clear that the downhill force is not equal to the weight force. Furthermore, a connection with the **angle of inclination α** must exist. For this, we look at the trigonometric relationships in a triangle. If you are no longer familiar with the relationships, you can fill in the gaps in your knowledge in chapter 2.5 Sine, cosine, tangent.

In the example this results in $\sin\alpha = \frac{F_a}{F_g} \rightarrow F_a = \sin\alpha \cdot F_g = \sin\alpha \cdot m \cdot g$

 The downward slope force acting on a body in the direction of the inclined plane is calculated as follows $F_a = \sin\alpha \cdot F_g = \sin\alpha \cdot m \cdot g$.

We can also verify the formula using the extreme cases. For an angle $\alpha = 90°$ the inclined plane is infinitely steep. The car would practically fall, so the weight force equals the slope down force. Fittingly, the sine of $\sin 90° = 1$, damit $F_a = F_g$.

The second extreme value is $\alpha = 0°$ which corresponds to a horizontal plane. The car is accelerated neither to the left nor to the right. Therefore, the resulting force must be $F_a = 0$ be. If we calculate the sine of $0°$, we see that the result is also zero $\sin 0° = 0$ and thus gives $F_a = \sin 0° \cdot F_g = 0$. So the formula also seems logically coherent.

We have already learned about the unit of acceleration. It is $\frac{m}{s^2}$. However, we have so far ignored one important property of all bodies, namely friction. We will include this in the next chapter.

4.9. Friction

We are familiar with friction from everyday life. What happens when the friction is no longer high enough, we see the impact when driving in winter on icy roads.

Friction is one of the most difficult effects in physics to describe. Since friction depends on countless factors, it is difficult to find a suitable model. But what is the best way to describe friction physically?

For this, we take a closer look at the properties of friction. We cannot simply push a car aside. "It's too heavy" is the colloquial expression. Strictly speaking, only the friction between tyre and road is too great. On a frozen lake, we can push a car under certain conditions. So we see that the greater the friction, the more force we have to use to move or accelerate an object.

Friction counteracts positive acceleration and amplifies negative acceleration.

Friction also depends on the surface properties of the materials that rub against each other. Using the example of the car, it is also clear that it depends on the mass, or the resulting weight force, or the normal force. F_g or the normal force F_N respectively.

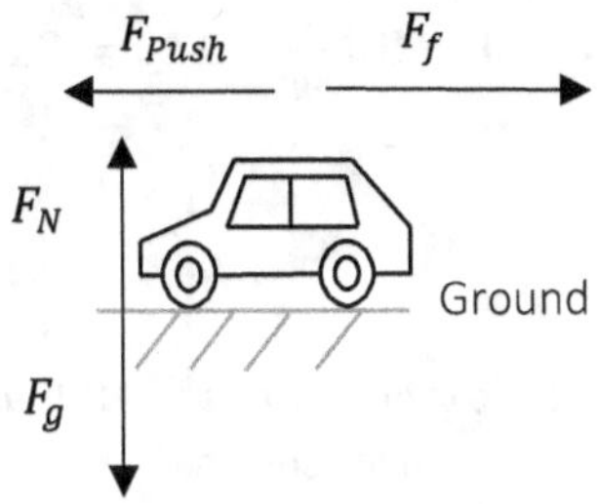

Figure 31: Frictional force on the car while driving

Since friction is complex, it is mostly determined by measurement. We increase the force F_{Push} that we have to exert on our car until it starts to move. We call this force friction force F_f. Then we put the force in relation to the normal force of the object. This gives us the **coefficient of friction**.

$$\mu = \frac{F_f}{F_N}$$

The **coefficient of friction** μ describes the ratio of frictional force and normal force. It is usually between zero and one. Exceptions are certain "anti-slip" coatings.

The value zero means that we do not have to overcome any frictional force and thus there is no friction. The value of one means that we have to apply the complete normal force. The value is determined by measurement.

To get a feel for the coefficients of friction, let's look at a table of common coefficients of friction.

Materials pair	Friction coefficient μ
Steel on steel	0.2
Wood on wood	0.5
Wood on stone	0.9
Steel on wood	0.5
Stone on stone	1
Steel on ice	0.03
Leather on metal	0.6

If we want to move a stone with a mass of m = 10 kg on a stone floor, we can use the following equation: $F_f = \mu \cdot F_N = \mu \cdot m \cdot g = 1.0 \cdot 9.81 \, \frac{N}{kg} \cdot 10 \, kg = \mathbf{91 \, N}$ raise.

How much force do we need to push a steel block with the mass $m = 1000 \, kg$ on a steel surface? How much force would we need on an ice surface?

Solution:

$$F_{Push} = F_R = \mu \cdot F_N = \mu \cdot m \cdot g = 0.2 \cdot 1000 \, kg \cdot 9.81 \, \frac{N}{kg} = 1{,}962 \, kN$$

On ice:

$$F_{Push} = F_R = \mu \cdot F_N = \mu \cdot m \cdot g = 0.03 \cdot 1000 \, kg \cdot 9.81 \, \frac{N}{kg} = 294.3 \, N$$

What is the maximum weight of a tree trunk (wood) that an adult man can pull across a wooden floor? The man can exert a maximum force of $F_{Push} = 800\ N$.

Solution:

$$F_{Push} = F_f = \mu \cdot F_N = \mu \cdot m \cdot g$$

$$m = \frac{F_{Push}}{g \cdot \mu} = \frac{800N}{9.81\ \frac{N}{kg} \cdot 0.5} = 163.1\ kg$$

We have learned about the force we have to exert to push an object. However, there is another frictional force, namely the one we have to apply constantly while the object is already in motion.

The initial force is always greater and is referred to as **static friction** or **static friction force**. Accordingly, the static friction coefficient is abbreviated as μ_s. In addition to this, there is the **sliding or kinetic friction** mentioned above and, analogously, the **kinetic friction coefficient** μ_k.

$F_{fs} = \mu_s \cdot F_N$ The force that we have to exert when pushing on something

$F_{fk} = \mu_k \cdot F_N$ The force we have to exert constantly when pushing

This expands the table of friction coefficients.

Materials pair	Static friction coefficient μ_s	Kinetic coefficient μ_k
Steel on steel	0.2	0.1
Wood on wood	0.5	0.4
Wood on stone	0.9	0.7
Steel on wood	0.5	0.4
Stone on stone	1	0.9
Steel on ice	0.03	0.01
Leather on metal	0.6	0.4

We can see that the static friction is always greater than the kinetic friction.

We have learned many basics about physical forces, including where they occur and how they work. Next, we will look at the relationship between different forces and energies and heat. To do this, we first need to understand what energy means and how we can tell energy and power apart.

5. Thermodynamics - Heat and Energy

Heat is intangible. We can perceive heat, but how can heat be described from a physical point of view?

To clarify this question, let's look at what heat actually is, how we can physically capture it and calculate with it.

5.1. The temperature

We are all familiar with temperature; it indicates the heat content of the environment. The physical quantity **temperature is** indicated by the formula sign T or ϑ abbreviated.

We measure temperature in **degrees Celsius °C.** Named after the Swedish astronomer Anders Celsius. Another unit of temperature is **degrees Fahrenheit °F,** named after the German physicist Daniel Fahrenheit.

Here, the temperature is always relative, i.e. it was determined at a reference temperature. For our temperature scale, we use the freezing point of water as a reference for 0 °C and the boiling point as a reference for 100 °C.

Daniel Fahrenheit used the lowest temperature he had ever measured (converted to approximately 17.4 °C) as the zero point (0 °F) and the body temperature of a human being as the reference for 96 °F.

The conversion from degrees Celsius to degrees Fahrenheit is linear, and therefore relatively simple.

$$\vartheta_{°C} = \frac{5}{9} \cdot (\vartheta_{°F} - 32) \ sowie \ \vartheta_{°F} = \frac{9}{5} \cdot \vartheta_{°C} + 32$$

For example, 20°C corresponds to $\frac{9}{5} \cdot 20 + 32 = 68\,°F$.

However, there is another very important temperature scale with the unit "degree Kelvin". This was named after "Lord Kelvin". It is the standard scale in physics. The reason for this is that it uses a very special reference.

To do this, let's first take a closer look at atoms at the molecular level. We notice that they themselves are constantly moving back and forth. The atoms are never still, but move within their connecting structures. These movements decrease with decreasing temperature. The atoms become slower and slower.

The temperature describes the energetic state of the atoms. The warmer it is, the faster the atoms move back and forth. It is a measure of the kinetic energy of the atoms.

If we keep reducing the temperature, the atoms move slower and slower.

At a temperature of **−273.15 °C absolute zero** is reached. Here, no atom moves any more.

The Kelvin temperature scale starts exactly there. It takes absolute zero, i.e. the point at which there is no movement and thus no energy, as the reference for 0 K. It uses the unit Kelvin K accordingly.

The temperature in space is relatively close to absolute zero. It is freezing cold there. There is a temperature of about 3 K.

A difference of one kelvin corresponds to a difference of one degree celsius, so that the temperature scale in kelvin is only shifted by 273.15 °C. In notation, the following is often used ϑ for a temperature indication in °C and T for a temperature indication in Kelvin.

$$\vartheta_{°C} = T_K + 273.15 \ \ sowie \ \ T_K = \vartheta_{°C} - 273.15$$

But: $\Delta\vartheta = \Delta T \rightarrow 100\,°C + 1\,K = 101\,°C$

Kelvin is also the SI unit of temperature. So we see that the unit kelvin is of great importance in physics.

5.2. Linear expansion

We have already learned that atoms move faster with increasing temperature. However, this is only half the truth. Because atoms not only move faster within their molecular structures, they also expand. Does that mean that everything expands in summer and contracts again in winter?

Indeed, yes, but it depends on the material. The characteristic property of the material is given in the coefficient of expansion. In order to determine this, the material is measured at a reference temperature, usually 20 °C.

It is then heated and the change in length is recorded.

$$\alpha = \frac{\Delta L}{\Delta T} \ \ \text{with } \Delta L: relative\ length\ change; \ \Delta T: temperature\ change$$

The coefficient of expansion α indicates the relative change in length of a substance. The unit is accordingly $\frac{1}{K}$ bzw. $\frac{1}{°C}$.

If we want to know the absolute change in length, we have to multiply the relative change by the length of the material. l_0

Iron has a coefficient of expansion of $\alpha = 1.2 \cdot 10^{-5} \frac{1}{K}$

This means that if the temperature rises by 40 °C between summer and winter, for example, iron expands in length by

$$\Delta L = \alpha \cdot \Delta T = 1.2 \cdot 10^{-5} \frac{1}{K} \cdot 40\ K = 4.8 \cdot 10^{-4} = 0.048\ \%\ \text{off.}$$

That doesn't sound like much at first. Let's calculate the absolute change in length. To do this, we take a 120 m long railway rail, as used for railway tracks. It expands accordingly by $\Delta l = \alpha \cdot \Delta T \cdot L_0 = 0.048\ \% \cdot 120\ m = 5.76\ cm$ expansion.

We see that $5.76\ cm$ can become a problem if suddenly screws no longer fit or there are gaps between the tracks.

In reality, of course, this linear expansion is taken into account. The rails are fixed so that they cannot expand freely. However, a resulting residual stress and possibly a deformation of the tracks remain.

Volume expansion

We can apply the same formulas used for linear expansion for volumetric expansion. We only have to replace the coefficient of linear expansion with the coefficient of volumetric expansion. This is often denoted by the index V for volume.

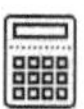

The coefficient of volume expansion of petrol is $\alpha_V = 0.00111 \frac{1}{K}$.

The petrol is pumped underground in a filling station at a temperature of

$T_0 = 8\ °C$. How does the volume of the petrol change when a car tank is filled with $V = 50\ l$ in the summer and the petrol then warms up?

$T_2 = 35\ °C$

Solution:

The temperature difference is $T_2 - T_1 = 27\ K$. The relative change results from:
$\alpha \cdot \Delta T = 0.00111\ \frac{1}{K} \cdot 27\ K = 0.03 = 3\ \%$

The absolute change results from

$$\Delta V = V_0 \cdot \alpha \cdot \Delta T = 0.00111 \, \tfrac{1}{K} \cdot 27 \, K \cdot 50 \, l = 3 \, \% \cdot 50 \, l = \mathbf{1,5 \, l.}$$

The total volume therefore corresponds to 51.5 l.

Another faux pas that is very often committed by technically unskilled people is the confusion of power and energy. Especially when it comes to renewable energies, terms are used incorrectly and inappropriate quantities and units are often mentioned, so that every physicist grabs their head in incomprehension. Therefore, the difference is explained below.

5.3. Work and Energy

The terms **energy and work** are used in physics for the same physical quantity. The energy or the work done is abbreviated with the formula symbol **E** or **W.**

Work describes the process of converting one form of energy into another. "Work is done when a heavy stone is lifted". Energy given refers to the stored work within a system. The stone has potential energy after being lifted. Practically and mathematically, the terms are to be used in the same way. The same units and formulae are used for calculation.

The work done is described as the product of the force acting over a distance.

$$W = F \cdot s$$

The work or the energy expended is independent of the time.

It does not matter whether we move a stone with a mass of $100 \, kg$ within one hour or within one minute. Only the distance covered counts. The work done in both cases is

$$\mathbf{W = F \cdot s.}$$

Work always acts on a body. The unit of work is Newton times metre $[W] = Nm.$

Unlike work, energy is not limited to work done on objects.

There are many different types of energy, for example heat energy. We can feel this when we touch a warm object. If it adds too much heat to our body, we suffer a burn. Furthermore, energy can take the form of movement. The kinetic energy indicates the energy of a moving body. Other forms of energy are, for example, electrical energy or rotational energy.

The SI unit of energy is the joule $[E] = J. \, 1J = 1 \, Nm$

Alternative units are watt-seconds Ws, or kilowatt-hours, kWh, when we're talking about electrical energy or heating energy. Naturalised units for energy are, for example, kilocalories, $kcal$. We use kilocalories to indicate the energy in our food.

In physical arithmetic, the various forms of energy hardly differ. All are expressed in joules, watt-seconds or kWh.

5.4. The difference between heat and temperature

There is often a lack of clarity among laypersons as to how the terms heat, temperature or work are distinguished. Therefore, we will eliminate all ambiguities. We have already got to know temperature. The same applies to energy or work. The physical quantity heat is abbreviated with the letter Q. Heat is a form of energy, which is why its unit is equal to the unit of energy $[Q] = J$.

In order to achieve a temperature increase, we must supply energy to a system in the form of heat. How much heat energy is needed depends on the substance and is described by the specific heat capacity c.

$$Q = c \cdot m \cdot \Delta T$$

The unit results from the equation and is accordingly $[c] = \dfrac{J}{kg \cdot K}$

With a heat capacity of $c = 1 \dfrac{J}{kg \cdot K}$ $1\,J$ energy is required to raise the temperature of the substance with a mass of $1\,kg$ by $1\,K$ or $1\,°C$ respectively.

Water has a specific heat capacity of $c_{H_2O} = 4.18 \dfrac{kJ}{kg \cdot K}$

How much energy do we need to heat a whirlpool with a water volume of $m = 15\,t$ from 20 °C to 40 °C? How many kWh is that? How much does the energy cost if one kWh costs 30 cents?

$$\text{Solution: } Q = c \cdot m \cdot \Delta T = 4.18 \dfrac{kJ}{kg \cdot K} \cdot 15{,}000\,kg \cdot 20\,K = 1.254\,GJ$$

$$1\,kWh = 1000\,W \cdot 3600s = 3.6\,MWs = 3.6\,MJ$$

So the heating requires $\dfrac{1.254 GJ}{3.6\,\frac{MJ}{kWh}} = 348.3\ kWh$. *Accordingly, at 30 cents per kWh,*

heating costs approximately $348.3\ kWh \cdot 0.3\ \dfrac{€}{kWh} = 104.5\ €.$

We now know what is behind energy. The amount of work we have to do. Often it is not only the total amount of work that is interesting, but also the time in which we have done it. This leads us directly to **power**.

5.5. Power P

Power (or performance) is a physical quantity and refers to the work that is done in a certain amount of time. Δt time.

$$P = \frac{\Delta W}{\Delta t}$$

The unit of power is the *watt* $[P] = W$, corresponding to *work per time*. The unit of work is the *joule*, the unit of time is the *second*.

One watt is therefore equivalent to one joule per second. $1\ \frac{J}{s} = 1\ W$.

On our electricity bill, the energy is stated in kWh, i.e. how many kW of power were used for how many hours.

Excursus: Horsepower

Another unit of power is the horsepower.

The unit horsepower goes back to James Watt. Horsepower described the average continuous performance of a working horse. It is unclear which horse and which power measurement was chosen as a reference. There are many assumptions, for example that James Watt used a pit horse as a yardstick. The horse pulled coal sacks out of the pits via ropes and pulleys. The working time, the weight of the coal sacks and the height lifted were used for calculation. 1 hp corresponds to approximately 735 W.

In the end, the horsepower was only able to establish itself with engine manufacturers. In physics, the watt, also named after James Watt, is used almost without exception.

When a service P over a period of time t is effective, a work is performed with $W = P \cdot t.$

A hair dryer has a power consumption of $2000\ W$ or $2\ kW$. If you let the hairdryer run for one second, the hairdryer consumes (this is actually not correct, because the energy is converted into moving heat and not "consumed") an energy of $2000\,W \cdot 1\,s = 2000\,Ws = 2\,kJ$.

After half an hour the hairdryer has used $2\,kW \cdot 0.5\,h = 1\,kWh$, after one hour it is $2\,kWh$ and so on. The power remains constant the whole time at $2\,kW$ but the energy depends on the time that has passed.

If one wants to convert J or kJ to kWh or vice versa, the following conversion applies:

$$1\,J = 1\,Ws = 1\,W \cdot \frac{1\,h}{3600\,s} = 2.8 \cdot 10^{-7}\,kWh = 0.00000028\,kWh$$

$$1\,kWh = 3600\,kWs = 3600\,kJ$$

Which units are correct, which are wrong? It is not a question of whether the numbers are correct, but only of the units!

In one hour, a refrigerator consumes $100\,W$.
Wrong - A refrigerator has a power consumption of $100\,W$. In one hour it consumes accordingly $100\,W \cdot 1\,h = 0.1\,kWh$.

Germany has an annual electricity demand of $550\,TWh$.
Correct - the energy demand is given in TWh.

The maximum demand for electrical power in Germany is approximately $80\,GWh$.
Wrong - The power is given in W. The correct answer is $80\,GW$.

A Tesla Model 3 has an engine power output of $360\,kW$ and a battery capacity of $75\,kWh$.

Both correct - the power is given in W ($360\,kW$ corresponds to approximately 490 hp), the energy stored by the battery in kWh. (The term battery capacity is not physically correct, as capacity is a different measure. Colloquially, it refers to the amount of energy stored.)

$100g$ of bread contains an energy of approx. $1\,MJ$ (one megajoule).
Correct - even though the unit joule is unusual for food, it is a form of energy. 1 MJ corresponds to about 240 kilocalories.

Herbert consumes 150 W while cycling. How much energy does he consume in two hours of cycling? How many kcal is that? $(1\ kWh\ =\ 860\ kcal)$

The energy results from the power times the effective time. Therefore in total 300 Wh = 0.3 kWh. This corresponds to 258 kcal. However, due to losses in converting the chemical energy from the food into kinetic energy, Herbert burns considerably more than 258 kcal in practice.

A trained young man can produce a continuous output of approximately 100 W or so. We recall that a pit horse can produce one horsepower, which is circa 735 W, which corresponds to approximately

5.6. Law of conservation of energy and efficiency

We have become a lot smarter and can distinguish between energy and power. Next, we look at another linguistic flaw when we talk about energy, the "consumption" of energy. The reason that we do not physically "consume" energy is explained by the **law of conservation of energy**.

The conservation of energy is one of the most fundamental laws of thermodynamics.

Most physical laws are to be regarded as "given by nature". One can go deeper and deeper into these laws until one arrives at the level of the smallest particles. As always, this book refrains from a detailed derivation and instead focuses on understanding and practical examples. This is also the case with the conservation of energy.

Conservation of energy states that there is a fixed amount of energy in the universe and that it cannot be destroyed or created. Energy can only be converted into different forms. We already know most of the forms, such as heat or kinetic energy.

For example, in a wind power plant, the kinetic energy of the wind is absorbed as rotational energy and then converted into electrical energy.

However, there is the restriction that every conversion results in a proportion of unusable energy, mostly in the form of **heat**. The ratio of how much energy is retained during a conversion and how much is lost is described by the efficiency.

Efficiency is a dimensionless quantity and is abbreviated with the Greek letter η (eta). η is defined as the ratio of the usable energy to total energy $\eta = \dfrac{E_{usefull}}{E_{not\,usefull}}$,

or, when converting energy, as the ratio of the usable energy after conversion to the energy before conversion. $\eta = \dfrac{E_{out}}{E_{in}}$.

You can quickly see that η is always between zero and one. Often η is given as a percentage. With an efficiency of exactly 1 (= 100 %), the entire energy is converted without loss. With an efficiency of zero, the complete energy can no longer be used after conversion.

The terms exergy and anergy are also often used in connection with the efficiency. Exergy describes the part of the energy that can be used.

In the case of driving, this is the proportion of energy that is converted into propulsion for movement; the waste heat, i.e. the heating of the engine, the unused energy, is referred to as anergy.

5.7. Examples of efficiency from everyday life

Photovoltaic modules today have an efficiency of about **20 %**. This means that only **one fifth of** solar energy is converted into electricity. This electricity must then be converted to the right voltage for the socket or stored, whereby losses in the range of **2-10 %** can occur.

LEDs convert about 40-50 % of the electrical power into light. The rest is needed by the control electronics to stabilise the current flow and is converted into heat. With conventional incandescent lamps, the colloquial light bulbs, the efficiency is significantly lower, here only 10-20 % of the energy is converted into light, the rest is released as heat.

However, a coal-fired power plant, which is supposed to convert the energy from the coal solely into electrical energy, generates over 60 % thermal energy, i.e. an efficiency of just under 40 %.

If several processes or conversions are carried out in succession, the total efficiency is obtained by multiplying the individual efficiencies.

Example: A wind turbine can convert 50 % of the kinetic energy of the wind into rotational energy. The speed is then increased via a gearbox. The gearbox has an efficiency of 95 %. The generator, which finally provides the electrical energy, has an efficiency of 90 %. The overall efficiency of the wind turbine is thus as follows

$$\eta_{ges} = n_1 \cdot \eta_2 \cdot \eta_3 = 0.5 \cdot 0.95 \cdot 0.9 = 0.4275 \text{ (corresponds to 42.75 \%).}$$

Efficiency is an important aspect when it comes to developing and promoting technologies. This is because it is often closely related to economic profitability.

However, the context must always be taken into account. Solar and wind energy is available in unlimited quantities and free of charge. Therefore, the efficiency of 20 % or 40 % is not a knock-out criterion for this technology. Gas or petrol, on the other hand, are raw materials and therefore have a market price, which is why you have to extract as much exergy as possible from the raw materials there in order to be able to operate profitably.

If we burn oil worth €100, at least €100 worth of electricity must be generated in the process. Every percent increase in efficiency goes directly into the economic balance.

Efficiency in electric and combustion engines:

We have already seen that good efficiency is extremely important in many technologies; mobility is no exception.

Nowadays, electromobility is becoming more and more popular. It is also high time that this development occurred. The change to sustainable mobility is essential and should be implemented as soon as possible. We will carry climate damage and environmental pollution with us for the rest of our lives.

However, we do not want to go too deeply into the ethical and ecological aspects of electric cars or internal combustion engines, instead we will look at both technologies from a physics perspective.

Electric motors are one of the most efficient inventions for locomotion. An electric motor converts about 90 % of the electrical energy into kinetic energy. Only 10% is emitted as waste heat. Traditional internal combustion engines, on the other hand, have an efficiency of 30-40 %. The technical maximum is around 45 %. Diesel and petrol engines differ only by a few percentage points.

This means that 30-40 % of the energy contained in the fuel is used to move the car. The remaining 60-70 % is given off as waste heat.

From a physical point of view, an internal combustion car is more like a heater, which moves as a by-product.

However, one must also consider that the energy density of petrol is much greater than that of today's battery storage systems. This means that internal combustion cars can still drive much further despite their poor efficiency, but they also consume considerably more energy in the process.

Next, we look at an example where different types of force or energy are converted into each other.

5.8. Spring force

Most people have seen a spring before. For example, the shock absorbers in a car or the inside of a biro. A spring in the physical sense is an elastic body that can be pulled apart or compressed. When no forces are acting on the spring, it is at **rest**. In order to deflect it from its rest position, i.e. to pull it apart or compress it, we have to apply a force.

For example, to be able to pull a metal spring apart, we have to pull firmly on it. The force is linearly dependent on the deflected distance. This means that if we pull a spring apart by 20 cm, we need twice as much force as if we only pull it apart by 10 cm.

The linear relationship between extension and force is also called **Hooke's (spring) law.** The force F that we have to exert to deflect a spring by the distance Δs *from* its rest position is calculated using:

$$F = D \cdot \Delta s$$

The proportionality constant D is called the spring constant, spring rate or spring stiffness. The value for D depends on the spring in question. Colloquially, we also use the terms hard and soft to describe the properties of a spring. A hard spring has a higher spring constant than a soft spring.

The unit of the spring constant is Newton per metre $[D] = \frac{N}{m}$. A spring constant of $1 \, \frac{N}{m}$ means that we have to apply a force of one newton to pull the spring apart or push it in by one metre.

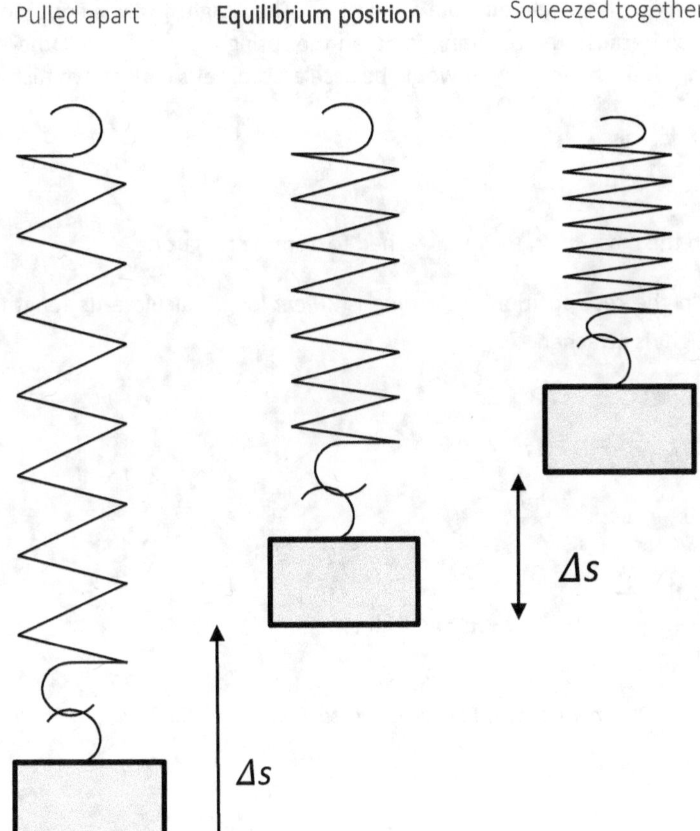

Figure 32: Spring in stretched, relaxed and compressed state

Strictly speaking, this is only correct for small displacements. If we compress the spring to the maximum, even more force will not bring more success. If we pull the spring apart, it will eventually be irreparably damaged. In the normal working range of a spring we can safely calculate with the equation $F = D \cdot \Delta s$ without hesitation. We call it a ideal spring.

Pulling a spring apart and compressing it are physically identical. It is not important whether we pull a spring apart by one metre or compress it.

> The force that the spring exerts against us is called the **restoring force.** It acts to restore the spring towards equilibrium.

According to Newton's third axiom, it is equal in magnitude but opposite in direction to the cause, i.e. $F_{Spring} = -D \cdot \Delta s$.

If we hang a weight on a spring, we can calculate its displacement. The force acting on the spring is calculated from $F_G = m \cdot g$. The weight force is equal to the spring force because the resulting force on the spring must be zero. Otherwise the spring would be $F = m \cdot a$ would be accelerated. Let's look at two tasks for this:

A sphere with the mass $m = 1\ kg$ is attached to a spring of hardness $D = 200\,\frac{N}{m}$. In the rest position the spring is 20 cm long. Calculate its length when the weight is attached.

Solution:

$$F_G = m \cdot g \; ; F_{Spring} = D \cdot \Delta s$$

$$m \cdot g = D \cdot \Delta s \rightarrow \Delta s = \frac{m \cdot g}{D}$$

$$\Delta s = \frac{1\ kg \cdot 9.81\ \frac{N}{kg}}{200\ \frac{N}{m}} = 0.04905\ m = 4.905\ cm$$

The spring is 24.905 cm long with the weight attached.

A bungee jumper with a mass of $m = 85\ kg$ hangs from the bungee cord. This stretches the rope from 10 m to 15 m.

Calculate the "spring hardness" of the bungee cord.

Solution:

$$F = D \cdot \Delta s \rightarrow D = \frac{F}{\Delta s} \rightarrow D = \frac{m \cdot g}{\Delta s} = \frac{85\ kg \cdot 8.91\ \frac{N}{kg}}{5\ m} = 166.77\ \frac{N}{m}$$

The person then jumps into the depths.

At the lowest point, the person is subjected to a spring force of $F = 2000$ N.

How long is the rope extended?

Thermodynamics - Heat and Energy

Solution:

$$F = D \cdot \Delta s \rightarrow \Delta s = \frac{F}{D} \rightarrow \Delta s = \frac{2000 \; N}{166.77 \; \frac{N}{m}} \approx 12 \; m$$

The rope is extended by 12 m. This makes it a total of 22 m long.

A spring exerts a force as soon as it is in the deflected state. If we compress a spring, it stores the energy expended. We have already learned about the energy or the work done. It is calculated as $W = F \cdot s$. Here, the question arises again as to which displacement we have to apply. At the beginning the displacement of the spring is zero, at the end it is exactly Δs. Analogous to the calculation of the uniform accelerated movement, we have to calculate the **average displacement of the spring.** $\bar{s} = \frac{1}{2} \Delta s$ be used.

The reason for this is that for a displacement of $\Delta s = 0$, no force has to be applied to compress the spring either. The more we compress the spring, the more force we have to apply. The average force is proportional to the average displacement. This is to be used for the stored energy.

Thus, the stored energy in a spring results in

$$E_S = \bar{F} \cdot s \text{ with } s = \Delta s \text{ and } \bar{F} = D \cdot \bar{s} = F = D \cdot \frac{1}{2} \Delta s$$

$$E_S = \frac{1}{2} D \cdot \Delta s^2$$

The energy is also called spring or tension energy.

A spring of hardness $D = 200 \; \frac{N}{m}$ is deflected by $\Delta s = 4 \; cm$ from its rest position. How much energy does the spring store? How much energy does it store if we double the displacement?

Solution:

$$E_S = \frac{1}{2} 200 \; \frac{N}{m} \cdot (0.04m)^2 = 0.32 \; J$$

If the displacement is doubled, the stored energy is quadrupled to $1.28 \; Joule$.

With this we have got to know our first concrete form of energy. Next, we will look at another form of energy that we may not yet have in mind as a concrete form of energy.

5.9. Kinetic energy

Kinetic energy describes the energy that a body carries with it, simply by the fact that it is moving. But why does a moving body have energy at all? Where does it come from?

To achieve the movement, we had to accelerate the body beforehand. To do this, we had to apply an acceleration a or a force F respectively. Since we used up the force over a certain distance s, work was done on the body.

This work done is calculated as $W = F \cdot s$ and is stored in the moving body in the form of **kinetic** energy. E_{kin}

In order to derive a formula for calculating the kinetic energy, we use the formulas that we have already looked at in the previous chapters. For the force F we insert $F = m \cdot a$. Since the force driving the body is constant, the acceleration a is also constant. It is therefore the case of a uniformly accelerated movement. Therefore, for the distance s we can insert the term: $s = \frac{1}{2} \cdot a \cdot t^2$ for the distance s. The exact derivation for uniformly accelerated movement was discussed in detail in chapter 4.7.

Together, the energy of a moving body results in

$$E_{kin} = F \cdot s = m \cdot a \cdot \frac{1}{2} \cdot a \cdot t^2 = \frac{1}{2} \cdot m \cdot a^2 \cdot t^2 = \frac{1}{2} \cdot m \cdot (a \cdot t)^2$$

$$E_{kin} = \frac{1}{2} \cdot m \cdot v^2$$

So we see that the kinetic energy is proportional to the mass of the body and quadratic to the speed of the body.

Let's take a look at a few calculation examples.

A car with a mass of $m = 1\,t$ which is moving at a speed of $v = 100\,\frac{km}{h}$ ($= 27.78\,\frac{m}{s}$) has a kinetic energy of

$$E_{kin} = \frac{1}{2} \cdot 1000\,kg \cdot \left(27.78\,\frac{m}{s}\right)^2 = 385{,}864\,kJ$$

A pedestrian with a mass of $m = 70\,kg$ and a speed of $v = 6\,\frac{km}{h}$ ($= 1{,}875\,\frac{m}{s}$) has a kinetic energy of only

$$E_{kin} = \frac{1}{2} \cdot 70\,kg \cdot \left(1{,}875\,\frac{m}{s}\right)^2 = 123\,J$$

Thermodynamics - Heat and Energy

5.10. Potential energy

Another form of energy is **potential energy**, also called position energy. We already know that work is done when we move an object a distance with a force, the abbreviation is E_{pot}.

However, there is a force acting on all of us that we have also already learned about, and that is gravity. The force of gravity or the acceleration due to gravity g is a constant force that pulls us towards the centre of the earth. When we move an object away from the centre of the earth, we have to do some work. $W = F \cdot s = m \cdot a \cdot s = m \cdot g \cdot s$ to be done. In the case of potential energy, we replace the distance s by the **height h** by which an object has been lifted.

Thus the potential energy of a body of mass m is given by

$$E_{pot} = m \cdot g \cdot h.$$

How much work must a climber with mass $m = 100\ kg$ do to climb the Zugspitze (Highest mountain in Germany) to a height of $h = 2962\ m$?

Solution:

$$E_{pot} = 100\ kg \cdot 9.81 \frac{N}{kg} \cdot 2962\ m = 2.906\ MJ$$

How many bananas would you have to eat for this, if one banana contains $89\ kcal\ (= 372\ kJ)$ and the climber can only utilise 30% of the energy using their muscles?

Solution: The usable energy of a banana is

$$E_{nutz} = 372\ kJ \cdot 0.3 = 111.6\ kJ$$

This means that the climber needs a total of

$$N_{Bananen} = \frac{E_{pot}}{E_{nutz}} = \frac{2{,}906 \cdot 10^6\ J}{111.6 \cdot 10^3\ J} = 26\ bananas$$

It takes 26 bananas to climb the Zugspitze.

With the help of the potential energy, we can also calculate the speed of a falling object. According to the conservation of energy, the total energy of a system remains the same. In free fall, therefore, all the potential energy is converted into kinetic energy. $E_{pot} = E_{kin}$

A sphere of mass $m = 1\ kg$ is dropped from a height $h = 10\ m$. With what speed does the ball hit the ground?

Solution: $E_{pot} = E_{kin} \rightarrow m \cdot g \cdot h = \frac{1}{2} \cdot m \cdot v^2$

$$v = \sqrt{2 \cdot g \cdot h}$$

$$v = \sqrt{2 \cdot 9.81\ \frac{m}{s^2} \cdot 10\ m} = \sqrt{196.2\ \frac{m^2}{s^2}} = 14\ \frac{m}{s} \approx 50\ \frac{km}{h}$$

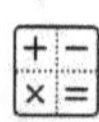

Alternatively, we could have calculated the speed using the formula for uniformly accelerated motion.

First we calculate the fall duration. To do this, we use the formula for the distance covered by a uniformly accelerated movement. The distance in this case is the height h and the acceleration a corresponds to the acceleration due to gravity g.

$$s = \frac{1}{2} \cdot a \cdot t_{Fall}^2 \rightarrow h = \frac{1}{2} \cdot g \cdot t_{Fall}^2 \rightarrow t_{Fall} = \sqrt{\frac{2\,h}{g}} = \sqrt{\frac{2 \cdot 10\ m}{9.81\ \frac{m}{s^2}}} \approx 1.43\ s$$

If we substitute the fall time into the velocity formula of uniformly accelerated motion, we get:

$$v = a \cdot t \rightarrow v = g \cdot t_{Fall} = 9.81\ \frac{m}{s^2} \cdot 1.43\ s = 14\ \frac{m}{s} \approx 50\ \frac{km}{h}$$

We see that there are two different approaches to the same task. The result is the same. That's what we expected.

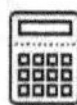

An apple with a mass of $m = 130\ g$ is ripe and falls from an apple tree onto the ground. It hits the ground with a speed of $7\ \frac{m}{s}$ on impact. How high is the tree? How fast would an apple twice as heavy hit the ground?

Solution: $E_{pot} = E_{kin} \rightarrow m \cdot g \cdot h = \frac{1}{2} \cdot m \cdot v^2$

$$\rightarrow h = \frac{1}{2} \cdot \frac{v^2}{g}$$

$$h = \frac{1}{2} \cdot \frac{\left(7\,\frac{m}{s}\right)^2}{9.81\,\frac{m}{s^2}} = 2.5\,m$$

The apple tree is 2.5 m high. The mass of the apple does not appear in the equation. An apple that weighs twice as much will also hit the ground with $7\,\frac{m}{s}$ impact.

With kinetic and potential energy, two more forms are added to our collection of different forms of energy. In the next chapter, we will see how different forms of movement merge into each other and create an oscillation.

5.11. Spring-mass oscillator

A **spring-mass oscillator** refers to the interaction of an ideal spring to which a mass m is attached. Often this experiment is also called a **spring pendulum.**

We have already calculated how much a spring expands when a weight is attached to it. In the example, the spring has reached a stable equilibrium phase. The spring force and the weight force just cancel each other out.

In the following experiment, we take a toy car and attach a spring to the left and right of the car. Both springs are equally hard, so they have the same spring constant D.

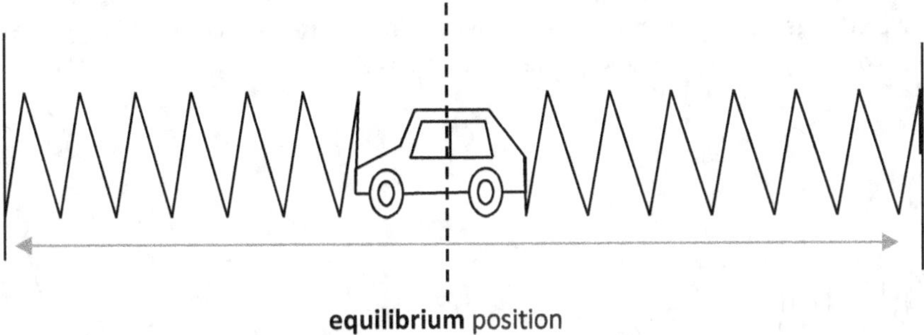

Figure 33: Car on the spring system in rest position

We then steer the car to the right from the equilibrium position. We refer to the displacement as $\hat{s}$. What happens when we let go of the car?

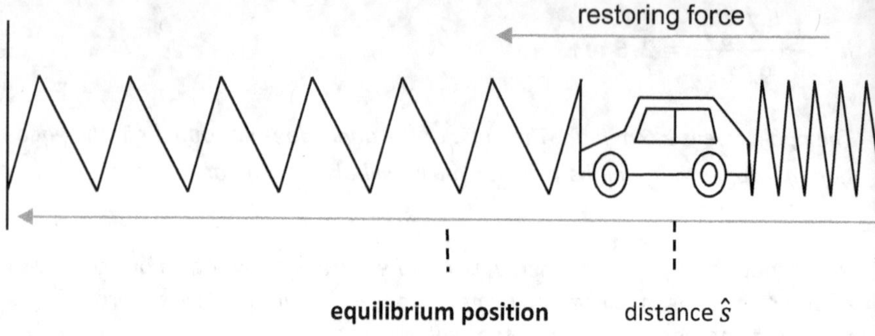

Figure 34: Deflected car on the suspension system

The right spring pushes the car towards the rest position, the left spring simultaneously pulls the car in the same direction. This accelerates the car according to $a = \dfrac{F}{m}$.

 In the process, the energy stored in the spring is converted into the kinetic energy of the car.

When the car reaches the equilibrium position, none of the springs exerts any force on the car. However, it has been accelerated to a speed $\hat{v}$. Therefore, it shoots to the left beyond the equilibrium position. There it must compress the left spring and pull the right spring apart. In the process, the car's kinetic energy is again stored in the springs. At the point $s = -\hat{s}$ the entire energy is stored in the springs and the game starts all over again. The car is accelerated and races beyond the resting position to the point of $s = \hat{s}$.

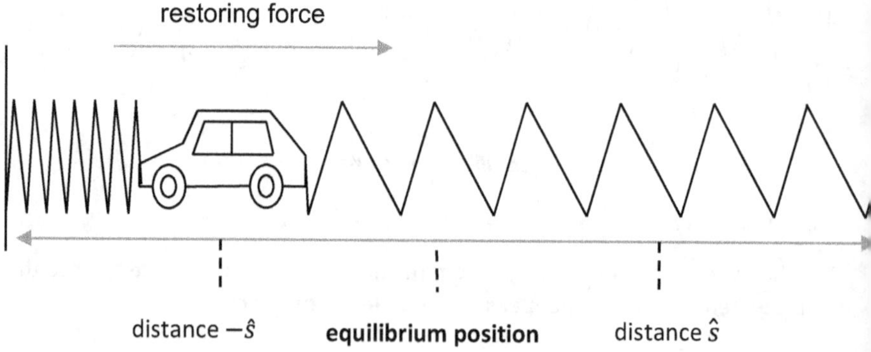

Figure 35: Car swings beyond the rest position

In reality, the car will never reach the starting point again, instead it will turn around before it does. The reason for this is friction. Both the friction of the tyres on the ground and the friction of the air take kinetic energy away from the car, thus slowing it down and preventing it from reaching full displacement again from its equilibrium position.

The interaction of tension and kinetic energy produces an oscillation of the displacement. $s(t)$.

We now know that an oscillation occurs, but what does it look like, how long does it last and how can we calculate the maximum speed of the car?

To do this, we take another look at the car's displacement over time. We also introduce a physical quantity called the **period.** It is abbreviated with a T *and* indicates the time that the car needs to arrive back at the starting point. A passage from $s = \hat{s}$ through the equilibrium position to $s = -\hat{s}$ and back again is called a **period.** For a "normalised cosine oscillation" the period is $T = 2\pi$ (see chapter 2.5. Sine, cosine, tangent).

T is given in seconds in practical tasks, such as our oscillation example. If the car needs 10 seconds to be pre-accelerated once, turn around and arrive back at the starting point, is $T = 10\ s$.

There are important points within the period.

At the time $t = 0\ s$ the car is at the start position, the displacement is $s(t) = \hat{s}$. At this time, the acceleration is maximum, the speed is just zero.

$$t = 0 \qquad s(t) = \hat{s} \qquad v(t) = 0 \qquad a(t) = \hat{a}$$

After a quarter of a period, the car crosses the equilibrium $s(t) = 0$. Since both springs are relaxed, the acceleration is also zero. However, it is going at the maximum speed.

We can carry out this line of thought for every significant point. As a temporal displacement we obtain a course, which is shown in the following graph.

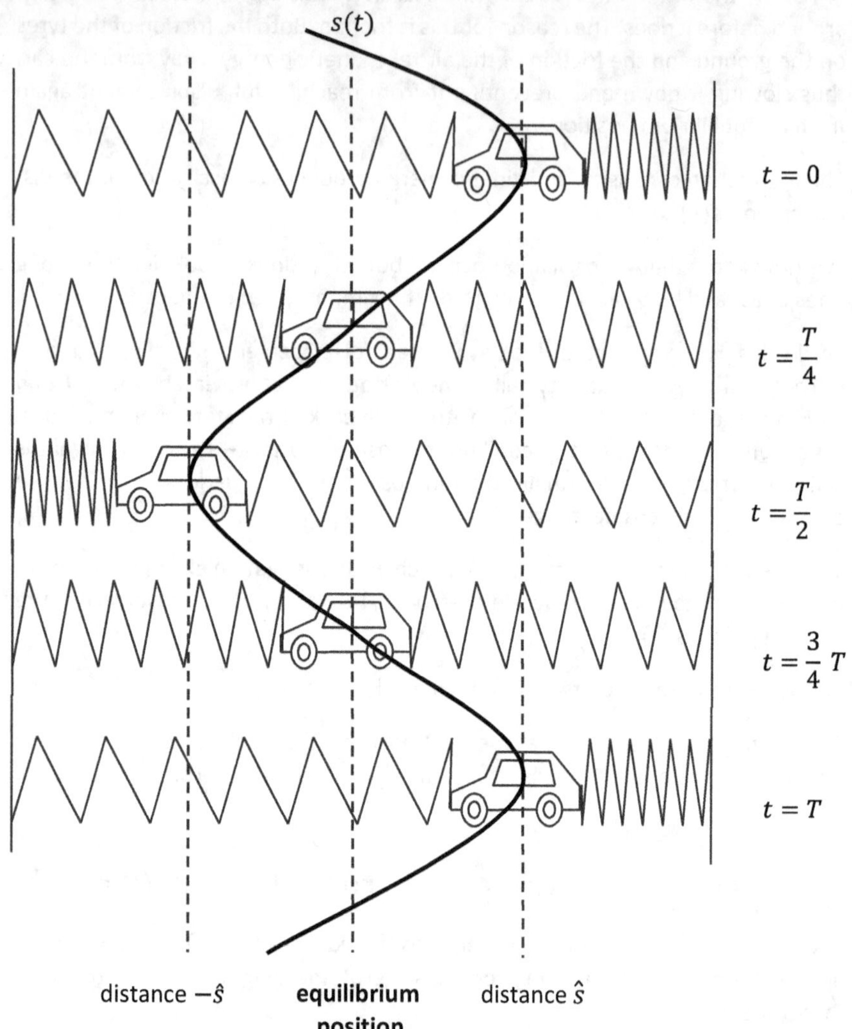

Figure 36: Cosine oscillation of the spring-mass system

Some of you may already recognise the curve. It is a *cosine curve* (see also chapter 2.5).

The maximum distance is called **amplitude**. The distance is measured from the zero point to the left or right.

The spring-mass system oscillates harmoniously with a displacement

$$s(t) = \hat{s} \cdot \cos{(2\pi \cdot f \cdot t)}.$$

Let's take a closer look at what the letter f inside the bracket is all about.

Before doing so, we can determine the oscillation mathematically.

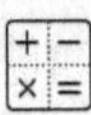

To do this, we set up a balance of forces, namely on one side of the accelerating force $F = m \cdot a$ and on the other side the corresponding spring force. $F = D \cdot s$. Since neither the displacement nor the velocity nor the acceleration are constant in the experiment, we replace them with the time-dependent quantities $s(t)$, $a(t)$ and $v(t)$.

We equate the accelerating force with the spring force and obtain

$$D \cdot s(t) = m \cdot a(t)$$

Next, it becomes very mathematical.

We know that acceleration describes the change over time $a = \frac{\Delta v}{\Delta t}$ for an arbitrarily small period of time, the span delta becomes a differential $\frac{dv}{dt}$ (see chapter 3.5).

The same applies to the speed. It is the differential of the distance.

$$v = \frac{ds}{dt}$$

This results in the acceleration being twice the differential of the path.

$$a = \frac{dv}{dt} = \frac{ds}{dt \cdot dt} = \frac{ds}{(dt)^2}$$

If we substitute the expression into the above equation, we get

$$D \cdot s(t) = m \cdot \frac{ds}{(dt)^2}$$

This is a differential equation, since both the differential of the path $\frac{ds}{dt}$ as well as the path itself is part of the equation. We need a function whose second, temporal change is equal to the function.

The detailed solution of the differential equation will be abbreviated in this book. The solution for the temporal displacement is also the cosine function, which we had already logically deduced earlier

$$s(t) = \hat{s} \cdot \cos\left(2\pi \cdot f \cdot t\right)$$

We have already learnt about the amplitude $\hat{s}$. But what does the new constant stand for? f is called **frequency** and indicates how many periods the car travels within one second. The unit of frequency is named after the German physicist Heinrich Hertz $[f] = \textbf{Hz}$. If the car drives forward once within one second, turns around and is accelerated back until it arrives at the starting point again, the frequency is $f = 1\,Hz$. Since it indicates how often an oscillation occurs per second, the frequency is just the reciprocal of the period duration and vice versa. $f = \frac{1}{T}; T = \frac{1}{f}$. The unit Hz *is* therefore equal to $\frac{1}{s}$. As an alternative to the frequency f, the **angular frequency** ω is often used. The angular frequency refers to a "normalised" cosine oscillation of 360° or 2π written as a radian.

$$\omega = 2\pi f$$

2π is a numerical value of ~6.28, therefore the unit of the angular frequency is also $\frac{1}{s}$.

One hertz corresponds to $\frac{1}{s}$ but the unit Hertz Hz is reserved exclusively for the frequency f. The angular frequency is therefore given in $\frac{1}{s}$ never in Hertz Hz.

If the car drives forward once within one second, turns around and is accelerated backwards until it arrives at the starting point again, the frequency will be

$f = 1\,Hz$ the angular frequency is $\omega = 2\pi f = 6.28\,\frac{1}{s}$.

The car performs two full periods in 5 seconds (forward-backward-forward-backward).

What is the period of the oscillation? At what frequency does the car oscillate? What is the angular frequency?

The period duration indicates the duration for one period. Therefore

$$T = \frac{5\,s}{2\,(Periods)} = 2.5\ s.$$

The frequency indicates the number of periods per second, therefore

$$\frac{2\,(Periods)}{5\,s} = 0.4\,Hz.$$

Alternative: $f = \frac{1}{T} = \frac{1}{2.5\,s} = 0.4\,Hz.$

$$\omega = 2\pi \cdot 0.4\ Hz \approx 2.5\,\frac{1}{s}$$

We now know what the frequency and period duration say. Let's take another look at our oscillation equation.

$$s(t) = \hat{s} \cdot \cos(2\pi \cdot f \cdot t)$$

If we want to know the position of the car after a certain time, we put the time into the vibration equation and get the position.

For example, if we steer the car around $\hat{s} = 10\ cm$ and the frequency of the vibration is $f = 0.4\ Hz$ we can solve the vibration equation by

$$s(t) = 10\ cm \cdot \cos(2\pi \cdot 0.4\ Hz \cdot t)$$

At the time $t = 0.5\ s$ is the position of the car:

$$s(0.5\ s) = 10\ cm \cdot \cos(2\pi \cdot 0.4\ Hz \cdot 0.5\ s)$$

$$= 10\ cm \cdot \cos(0.4\pi)$$

$$= 10\ cm \cdot 0.3 = 3\ cm$$

After 0.5 seconds the car is at the position $s(0.5\ s) = 3\ cm$

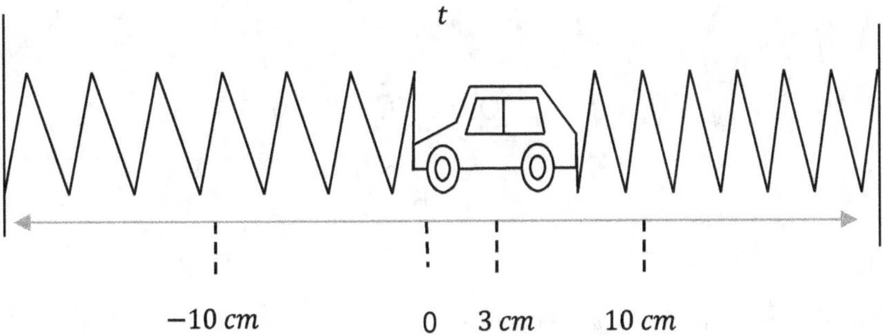

Figure 37: Position of the car after half a second

The same consideration that we made for the position of the car can be applied to its speed $v(t)$.

In the beginning, the speed of the car $v(0\ s) = 0$.

In the zero crossing, i.e. for the first time after a quarter period, the speed is maximum $v\left(\frac{T}{4}\right) = \hat{v}$.

The equation for the velocity is analogous to the position determination and is only shifted by a quarter period.

The sine is shifted by a quarter period compared to the cosine.

The period duration and thus also the frequency of the oscillation is the same.

Therefore, the vibration equation that gives us the instantaneous velocity of the car is: $v(t) = \hat{v} \cdot \sin(2\pi \cdot f \cdot t)$.

Let's check the equation by taking the values $t = \frac{T}{4}$ and $t = \frac{T}{2}$ in the equation. How fast is the car after a quarter of the period and after a half of the period?

$$v\left(\frac{T}{4}\right) = \hat{v} \cdot \sin\left(2\pi \cdot f \cdot \frac{T}{4}\right) = \hat{v} \cdot \sin\left(2\pi \cdot \frac{1}{T} \cdot \frac{T}{4}\right) = \hat{v} \cdot \sin\left(\frac{\pi}{2}\right) = \hat{v} \cdot 1 = \hat{v}$$

$$v\left(\frac{T}{2}\right) = \hat{v} \cdot \sin\left(2\pi \cdot f \cdot \frac{T}{2}\right) = \hat{v} \cdot \sin\left(2\pi \cdot \frac{1}{T} \cdot \frac{T}{2}\right) = \hat{v} \cdot \sin(\pi) = \hat{v} \cdot 0 = 0$$

After a quarter of a period, the speed is at a maximum. This is logical, because that is exactly what we set as a condition to derive the equation.

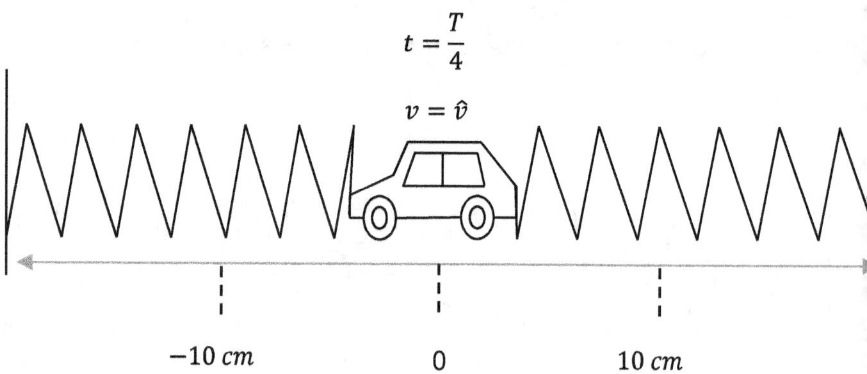

Figure 38: Position of the car after a quarter of a period

After half a period, the car is exactly at the reversal point at $s = -\hat{s}$. The speed there is zero. We can determine the position and the speed of the car for every point in time. All we need is the frequency of the oscillation and the amplitudes of the distance and speed.

The maximum speed $\hat{v}$ depends on how long the car can be accelerated, i.e. how much it is deflected at the beginning. It also depends on the frequency of the oscillation.

Thermodynamics - Heat and Energy

The context is $\hat{v} = \hat{s} \cdot \omega = \hat{s} \cdot 2\pi \cdot f$.

But how do we arrive at the frequency of the oscillation? To do this, we consider what the frequency, i.e. how fast the car vibrates, depends on. First of all, it is clear that it depends on the selection of the springs used, i.e. the spring stiffness D. Harder springs can accelerate the car more, so it vibrates faster.

Another influencing factor is the mass of the car. A heavy car is accelerated more slowly, it therefore vibrates more slowly.

 The frequency, or the angular frequency of the oscillation, is determined by the hardness of the spring and the mass of the oscillating object.

The exact relationship of the quantities is as follows:

$$\omega = 2\pi f = \sqrt{\frac{D}{m}}$$

Let's go through the new formulas with concrete examples and numerical values.

A car with the mass m = 0.5 kg which is attached to two springs with the total spring hardness $D = 4.5\frac{N}{m}$ vibrates with a (circular) frequency of

$$\omega = 2\pi f = \sqrt{\frac{4.5\frac{N}{m}}{0.5\ kg}} = 3\frac{1}{s} \rightarrow f = \frac{\omega}{2\pi} = \frac{3}{2\pi}\frac{1}{s} = 0.477\ Hz$$

The period of the oscillation is $T = \frac{1}{f} = \frac{1}{0.477\ Hz} = 2.1\ s.$

 It does not matter whether the car is deflected by 1cm, 5cm or 10cm, the duration of the oscillation is independent of the displacement!

Let's look at another example of vibration.

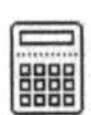

A stone of the mass m = 100g is hung on a rubber rope with a spring hardness $D = 10\ \frac{N}{m}$ and deflected by $\hat{s} = 20cm$. At what (circular) frequency does the stone vibrate? What is the equation of oscillation for the distance and the speed? Where is the stone after $t = 3s$?

For the task, the influence of gravity can be neglected.

$$\omega = \sqrt{\frac{D}{m}} = \sqrt{\frac{100\,\frac{N}{m}}{0.1\,kg}} = 10\,\frac{1}{s}\,;\, f = \frac{\omega}{2\pi} = \frac{10\,\frac{1}{s}}{2\pi} = 1.6\,Hz$$

The maximum speed results from:

$$\hat{v} = \omega \cdot \hat{s} = 10\,\frac{1}{s} \cdot 20\,cm = 2\,\frac{m}{s}$$

The vibration equations and concrete values can thus be calculated using the following formulae:

$$s(t) = 20\,cm \cdot \cos\left(10\,\tfrac{1}{s} \cdot t\right) \qquad s(3\,s) = 20\,cm \cdot \cos\left(10\,\tfrac{1}{s} \cdot 3\,s\right) = 3\,cm$$

$$v(t) = 2\,\tfrac{m}{s} \cdot \sin\left(10\,\tfrac{1}{s} \cdot t\right) \qquad v(3\,s) = 2\,\tfrac{m}{s} \cdot \sin\left(10\,\tfrac{1}{s} \cdot 3\,s\right) = -1.97\,\tfrac{m}{s}$$

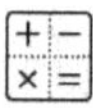

Real systems

We have already learned that there is virtually no system without friction. In an oscillation, friction ensures that the amplitude decreases over time. The oscillation subsides. That is why we call this type of oscillation damped oscillation.

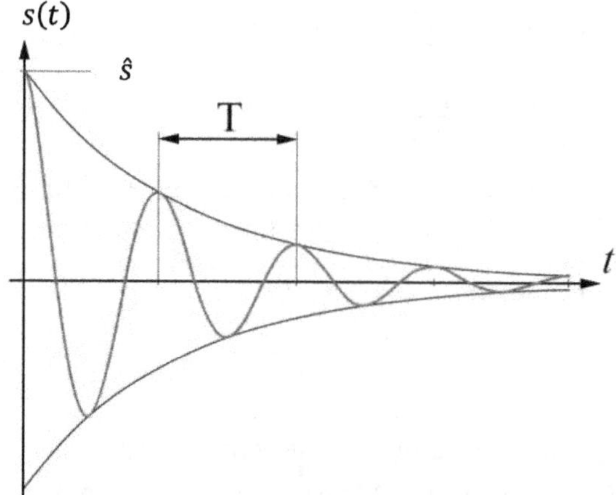

Figure 39: Decaying oscillation

This concludes the chapter on spring-mass oscillators. In this chapter we have learned what the physical quantities period, frequency and angular frequency mean and how we can represent an oscillation analytically. We will also encounter these quantities in the coming chapters because oscillations cannot only occur mechanically.

Electromagnetic oscillations enable us to navigate via GPS, make phone calls or send a message via our smartphone while on the move. Before we get to electromagnetic waves, we will first learn the basics of electrical engineering. We will look at the systematics of the behaviour of an electron, the structure of permanent magnets and electro-magnetism.

6. Electrical engineering - current, voltage and co

The following chapter was largely taken from the book "Electrical Engineering without Prior Knowledge". However, simplifications and changes have been made so that the chapter remains consistent with the content of this book.

If you are new to the subject of electrical engineering, many of the terms used are abstract and difficult to imagine. It takes time and practice to define the terms and classify them correctly. To make it easier to remember the terms, we use a model.

 A model is a **simplification of reality** and attempts to map new, complex facts onto what is already known.

In our case, many analogies can be used to transfer the topic of the electric circuit to a familiar **water circuit.**

6.1. The stream-water model

Each component in the water circuit is contrasted with a corresponding component from the electricity circuit:

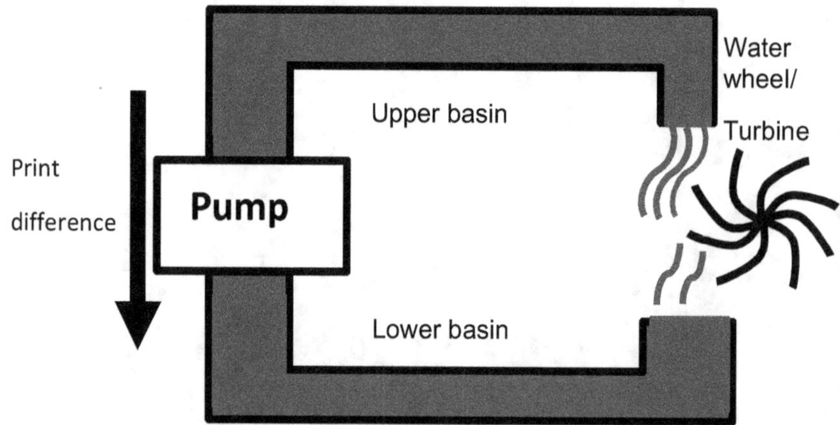

Figure 40: Water cycle

In simple terms, a water circuit consists of two water basins, a water pump, pipes that transport the water and a consumer, such as a turbine, a water wheel or similar.

One water basin is **higher** than the other. The pump constantly pumps water upwards. As a result, the water in the upper basin has a greater potential energy. There is a pressure difference between the upper and the lower basin.

The water runs **through the pipes** and via the consumer back into the lower basin. The consumer is driven by the moving water. The water thus transmits the **energy of the pump to** the consumer. For each element in the water circuit, we look for a corresponding element in the electric circuit.

Let's start with our pipes through which the water flows. In the electric circuit, these are the **cables or wires** through which the current flows. The water in the water circuit corresponds to our current, which consists of **moving electrons.** But how is a conductor actually constructed and how can the electrons move in it? Let's take a very close look at the material.

6.2. Atoms, electrons, protons

In order to understand the various effects of electrical engineering, let's first take a look at the basic building blocks of physics - atoms. Every material consists of atoms at the smallest level. An atom consists of positively charged particles, the **protons**, particles without charge, the **neutrons,** and negatively charged particles, the **electrons.**

The formula symbol of the **charge is Q** and the unit of the charge is the **coulomb C.** In SI units $1\,C = 1\,A \cdot 1\,s = As$. The charge is therefore given in C or As.

The **elementary particles** (protons and electrons) both have the smallest possible charge that is physically possible. This is called the **elementary charge** and is abbreviated as e.

The elementary charge has the value of $e = \mathbf{1.602 \cdot 10^{-19}}$ coulomb. An electron has the charge of $Q = -e$ and a proton has a charge of $Q = +e$.

Since the charge of an atom is neutral overall, it has the same **number of electrons as protons.** The protons and neutrons form the atomic nucleus, while the electrons race around the nucleus at the speed of light. Almost the entire mass of the atom is united in the atomic nucleus.

Each element such as hydrogen, oxygen, carbon, iron or even nickel, copper and zinc have a very specific, unique number of protons and electrons that hold the element together.

If we look at the structure of an atom in more detail, we see that the electrons do not race randomly around the atomic nucleus, but travel along defined paths, so-called orbitals.

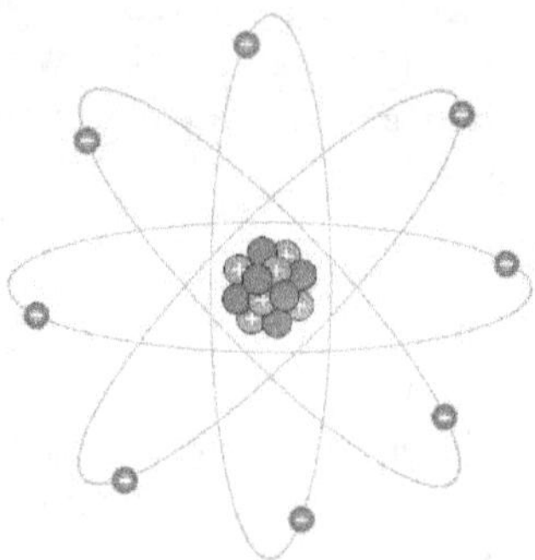

Figure 41: Structure of an atomic model

These are called **shells**, which can hold different numbers of electrons. The innermost shell (K-shell), which is close to the nucleus, can hold only two electrons; the second (L-shell) can hold a full **8 electrons, the** third (M-shell) up to **18 electrons** and so on. In total, there are up to **seven shells,** depending on how many protons and thus how many electrons an atom has.

If an atom has only 2 electrons, only the first shell is filled. If it has 11 electrons, the first and second shells are completely filled and there is a single electron in the third.

6.3. Why do some materials conduct electricity?

Electricity consists of nothing but moving charge carriers. A material is therefore a good conductor if the charge carriers can move easily. Since the protons are fixed in the nucleus, only the electrons remain, which can move freely, but they are attracted by the positive nucleus.

Since the electrons on the outer shells are not attracted as strongly, they can detach from the atomic nucleus more easily.

 The electrons on the outer shells are therefore very important for the conductivity of a substance.

The electrons that lie on the outermost shell are also called **valence electrons.**

Metals such as iron, copper or aluminium form a special lattice structure in which the valence electrons can **move freely.**

 In metals, the valence electrons buzz around like a homogeneous gas in the lattice; one also speaks of an **electron cloud** or **electron gas** in the metal.

Non-conductive materials, such as most plastics, do not form a lattice and strongly retain their valence electrons. This means that electrons cannot flow through the material.

What we generally know as electricity is nothing more than the movement of valence electrons from A to B.

 **A current flow consists of moving charge carriers**

Let us return to our water model. The valence electrons are freely movable and therefore correspond to water in the water cycle. These transfer charges, or the energy in the circuit. Next, we come to the **pressure difference** between the basins. This is caused by gravity, mathematically speaking by the **earth's gravitational field**. We find the electric **field** in the circuit.

6.4. The electric field E

First, let's clarify the properties of the Earth's **gravitational field.** It ensures that everything on this planet experiences an **attraction towards the centre of the Earth.** The principle behind this is that masses attract each other. The larger the masses and the closer they are to each other, the stronger the force of attraction.

In our water cycle, this means that the water can drive the turbine because it was pumped up by the pump, i.e. it was lifted against gravity or the earth's gravitational field. Physically speaking, work has been done and potential energy has been supplied to the water. This has created a pressure difference. When the water flows down the pipes, the pressure is converted at the consumer (the turbine).

In electrical engineering, there are **electric** and **magnetic fields** that assign **potentials** to electrons. But what is a field and how can you imagine it?

6.5. Representation of E-fields

First of all, every field has a cause. In the case of the electric field or simply **E-field,** the cause is charged particles.

 **Electric fields form around charged particles.**

An accumulation of positive charge is called a **positive pole, an** accumulation of negative charge carries correspondingly a **negative pole.**

In order to be able to represent the field, it is necessary to draw field lines that start at the **cause**.

 Field lines always point away from a positive charge and towards a negative charge. The density of the field lines indicates the strength of the field.

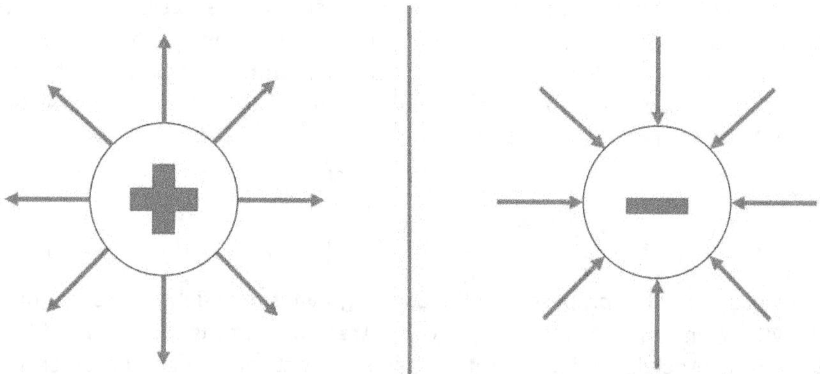

Figure 42: Field lines of a point charge

The illustration shows that the field lines (light blue arrows) are clearly closer together (denser) at the circle representing the point charge than those farther away from it. This means that the field is correspondingly stronger there.

If several charge carriers meet, a wide variety of field lines are created.

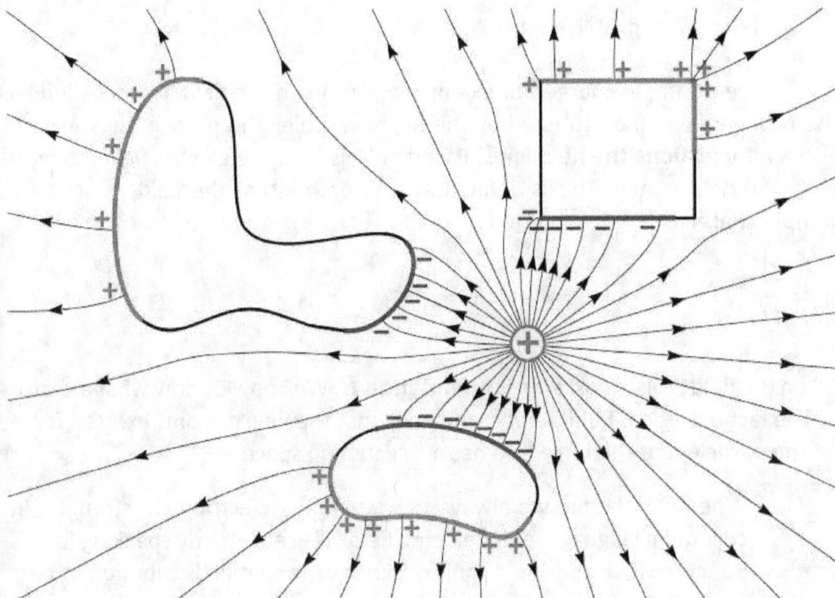

Figure 43: Electric field lines

The field lines are jumbled and do not seem to follow any order.

If, on the other hand, the field lines are parallel, we speak of a **homogeneous field**. The field has the **same value** at every point. This is the case, for example, if we have two plane opposing metal plates on which charge carriers are placed.

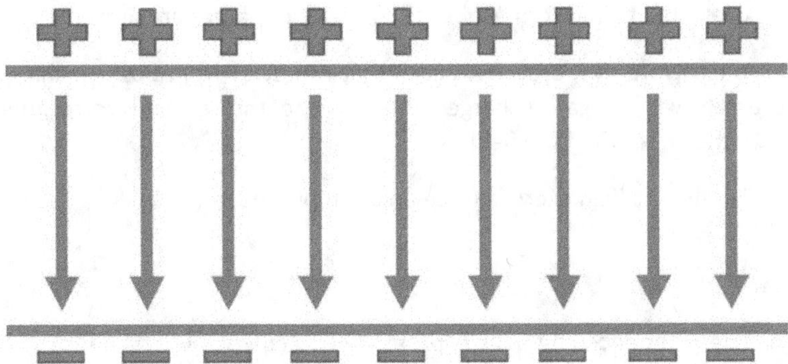

Figure 44: Homogeneous electric field

6.6. The force in the electric field

If we place a **sample charge,** for example a proton, in the field, it is repelled by the positive pole and attracted by the negative pole. The particle thus experiences a **force along the field lines**. Based on this fact, the electric field strength E can be determined. This is defined as the force F that the field exerts on a **sample charge Q.**

$$E = \frac{F}{Q}$$

Often the field is also found in **vector notation $\vec{E}$**. We know by now what a vector is. The fact that the E-field is a vector means that the field not only exerts a force on the particle, but the force also has a direction in space.

 When calculating, we always talk about the electric field strength. In colloquial language, only "electric field" is used. Strictly speaking, this is not correct, as the "field" only describes the spatial distribution, not its strength.

The unit of the electric field strength results from

$$[E] = \frac{N}{C} = \frac{kg}{m^2 \cdot As}$$ another unit for the strength of the electric field is volts per metre. $\frac{V}{m}$.

Summary of an electric field:

 An electric field is formed wherever electric charges are present.

 To illustrate this, draw field lines that run away from positive charges and towards negative charges. The density of the field lines corresponds to the strength of the field.

 The electric field exerts a force on a sample charge.

What force is experienced by a single proton with a charge of

$$Q = 1.602 \cdot 10^{-19}\ C \text{ in an E-field with } E = 3 \cdot 10^9\ \frac{N}{C}?$$

Solution: $E = \frac{F}{Q}$; $F = E \cdot Q = 3 \cdot 10^9\ \frac{N}{C} \cdot 1.602 \cdot 10^{-19}\ C = 4.8 \cdot 10^{-10}\ N$

$$= 480 \, pN \, (Pikonewton)$$

What force does an electron experience in the same E-field? What is the difference?

*Solution: A proton has **the same** charge as an electron, but a different sign. Therefore, the force is the same for the electron, but with a negative sign (-480 pN). The proton is accelerated in the opposite direction.*

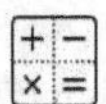

Excursus equipotential lines:

In more in-depth literature, equipotential lines are also often mentioned. These are **perpendicular to the electric field lines.**

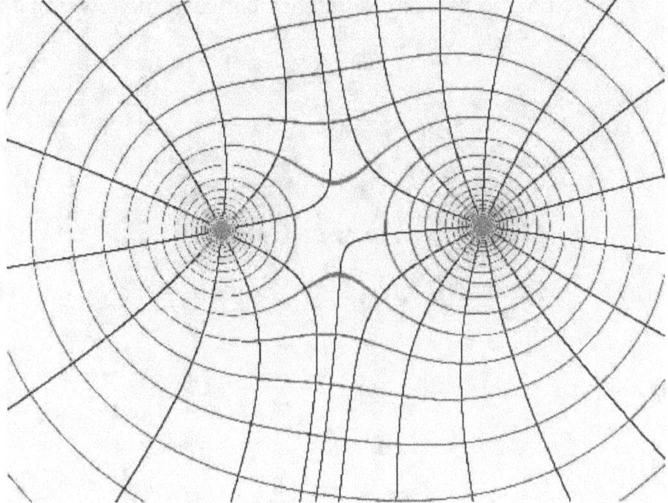

Figure 45: Equipotential lines

The dark lines are the field lines of the point charges. The ellipses represent the equipotential lines. At the **crossing points, the** equipotential and E field lines are **perpendicular to each other**. The same electric potential prevails at each point. In order to understand the meaning of the equipotential lines, we first learn about the electric potential and the voltage U.

6.7. The electrical potential and the voltage U

The electric potential or electrostatic potential is abbreviated with φ (Greek lower case letter Phi). It has the unit **volt V.**

The electric potential describes the potential energy of a sample charge within an electric field. The electric field assigns a potential to every point in space.

Analogously in the water cycle, it is the absolute pressure that the water possesses and exerts through height. The pressure exerted by the basin of water at a certain height is determined by the earth's gravitational field. As a simplified example, the upper basin has a gravity pressure of one bar and the lower basin has a pressure of zero bar.

However, in the water circuit it is not the absolute pressures that matter, but only the relative pressure, i.e. the pressure difference between the lower and upper water basin.

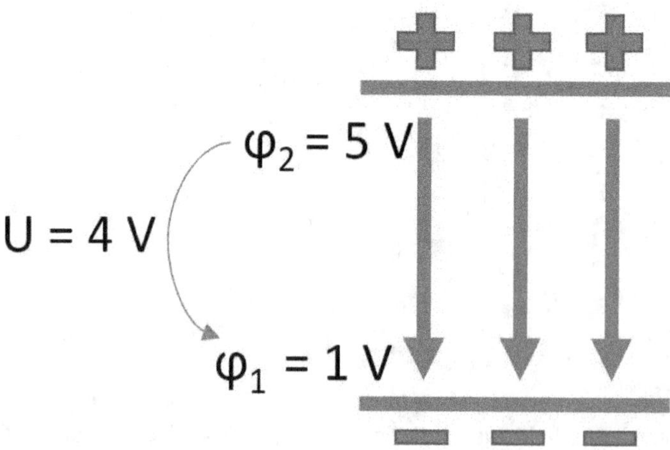

Figure 46: Potentials and voltage in the homogeneous E-field

The difference between two potentials φ2-φ1 is called the **voltage U**, the voltage also has the unit volt V.

With a voltage, it must always be ensured that it only indicates a **potential difference.** Therefore, you always need a reference potential.

Electrical engineering - current, voltage and co

But what exactly is our pump now? The pump in the water circuit corresponds to a **voltage source** in the electricity circuit. A voltage source is, for example, a **battery**. A standard AA battery has a **voltage of 1.5 V**. This means that the positive pole, i.e. the upper contact point of the battery, has an electrical potential that is 1.5 V higher than the negative pole.

The circuit symbol of a voltage source is a circle with a solid line. Every voltage source consists of a positive and a negative pole. An ideal voltage source generates a voltage independent of the applied load. In reality, this is only approximately possible.

In electrical circuits, one usually selects the **lowest potential** and defines it as the **reference potential.** This means that it has the potential of $\varphi = 0$ V and all other potentials are specified in relation to this potential.

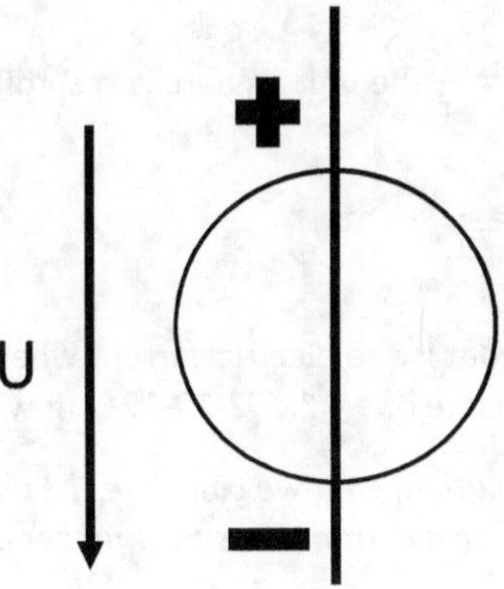

Figure 47: Circuit symbol of a voltage source

In electrical engineering, voltages are relevant almost without exception. Potentials are hardly ever considered, as current can only flow at a potential difference.

6.8. The current I

We have already learned that the water in the water cycle corresponds to our electrons. But in everyday life we always talk about **currents**, i.e. **moving electrons**. A measure of the strength of the electron flow is therefore the current, abbreviated with the formula symbol I. Its unit is the **ampere A**. Since the current indicates the flow of electrons, and each electron has a charge, the current indicates how much **charge** is transferred **per time.**

$$I = \frac{Q}{t} \text{ the unit ampere is accordingly } 1\,A = 1\frac{C}{s}$$

What is the electric current when one quadrillion (10^{15}) electrons, each with a charge of e = 1.602·10-19 C, flow in a conductor per second?

Solution: First we calculate the charge. The total charge results from the charge of an electron times the number of electrons.

$$Q = n \cdot e = 10^{15} \cdot 1.602 \cdot 10^{-19}\,C = 1.602 \cdot 10^{-4}\,C = 160.2\,\mu C$$

Then we look at the time in which this charge flowed.

$$I = \frac{Q}{t} = 160.2\,\frac{\mu C}{1s} = 160.2\,\mu A$$

Power sources:

Analogous to voltage sources, there are also **current sources.** These do not generate a potential difference, but a **constant current I,** independent of the voltage U applied.

In the water cycle, we can think of a power source as a pump that always produces a constant amount of water flow, so it only drives the water, but does not raise it or increase the pressure.

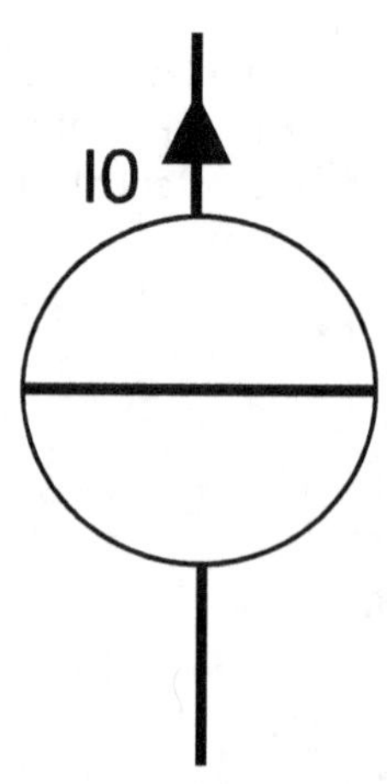

Figure 48: Switching symbol of a current source

Electrical engineering - current, voltage and co

6.9. Technical and physical current direction

In electrical engineering, as well as all other engineering sciences, one uses the technical direction of current, but what does that mean exactly?

Let's start with the physical direction of the current. We know that electrons are negative charge carriers that form the current flow. Therefore, the current flows from where there are more electrons to where there are fewer electrons. Since electrons are negatively charged, the current flows from the negative pole to the positive pole. This is the "physical" direction of current or the direction of flow of the electrons.

The term "physical current direction" is somewhat misleading, since in physics the technical current calculation is usually also used. The "physical current direction" merely corresponds to the direction of movement of the electrons, not the direction actually used in electrical engineering.

However, the current and its properties were discovered before it was known exactly whether the positive or negative charge carriers were responsible for the current flow. It was wrongly assumed that the positive charge carriers, i.e. the protons, form the current flow. In this model, the current flows from the positive pole to the negative pole. This notation has been retained until today. Nothing changes in the calculations, the effects etc. It is only good to know that the current flow is different in reality from the way we draw it.

The technical current direction is used in all circuit diagrams, drawings and circuits.

In order to avoid getting confused, let's remember:

In a technical circuit, the current always flows from the positive pole to the negative pole!

6.10. The magnetic field

Just like the gravitational field, the **magnetic field is** familiar from our everyday lives. Everyone is familiar with magnets, for example for attaching notes to a pin board. Since these magnets are **permanently magnetic**, they are also called **permanent magnets.**

There are many similarities and analogies between magnetic and electric fields. At the end of the chapter, we therefore compare the magnetic and electric fields again.

 The **magnetic field strength** has the formula symbol H, since it also has a direction, just like the electric field, it is often described as $\vec{H}$ described. The unit of the magnetic field is $\frac{A}{m}$.

Often, it is not the absolute magnetic field that is needed, but **the magnetic flux density $\vec{B}$** . It indicates how **strong the magnetic flux** is in the magnetic field. It also indicates the force acting on a sample charge.

We are not interested in the complete magnetic field of a body, but only in the "effects", and this is described by the flux density.

 You can imagine the magnetic field like a waterfall. We are not interested in the complete extent and size of the waterfall, but only in the flux density of the falling water.

 The magnetic field strength $\vec{H}$ is less important in technology. Almost without exception, flux density is used for $\vec{B}$ calculated.

Therefore, the abbreviation for the magnetic field is generally referred to as a **B-field** (analogous to the **E-field** - the electric field).

The unit of magnetic flux density is the **Tesla T**, or Newton per ampere and per metre. $1\,T = 1\frac{N}{A \cdot m}$

The magnetic flux density and the magnetic field are directly related via the permeability μ. μ is therefore also often called magnetic conductivity.

$$\vec{B} = \mu_0 \mu_r \times \vec{H}$$

$$\mu_0 = Permeabilty\ in\ vacuum = 1{,}257 \times 10^{-6}\frac{Vs}{Am}$$

$$\mu_r = Substance - dependent\ permeability$$

Common **permeabilities** μ_r are, for example, iron or ferrite with μ_r of 15,000.

Now that we have learned about the physical quantities, we come to the cause of a B-field. An electric field is created when charged particles form a positive and a negative pole.

 The cause of the magnetic field in a permanent magnet is not charged particles, but so-called **elementary magnets.**

6.11. Elementary magnets

This is again a physical model. Each element consists of **countless** small elementary magnets. These elementary magnets cannot be broken apart because they represent the smallest unit. Just like a "large" magnet, they consist of a north and a south pole. Equal poles repel each other, different poles attract each other.

In most materials, these elementary magnets are arranged without a system. The respective poles neutralise each other and the material is not magnetic.

Ordered - magnetic   Without system - non-magnetic

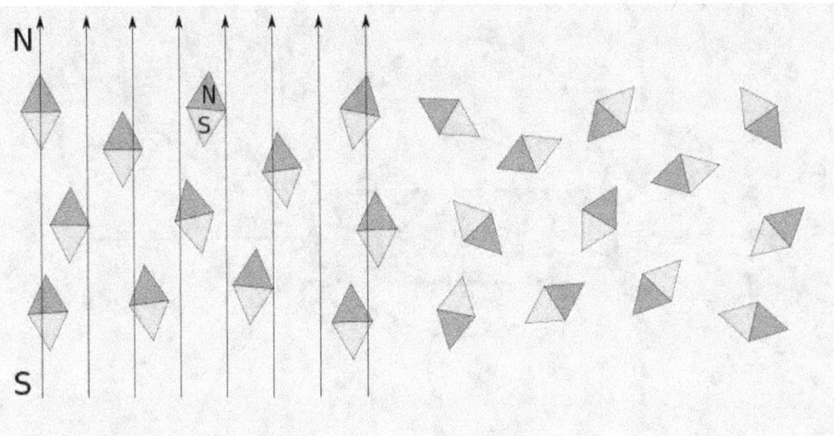

Figure 49: Elementary magnets

It is different with magnetic materials. There, all the elementary magnets are aligned. This creates a north and a south pole: the material is magnetic. The best-known magnets are **neodymium magnets**. These are made from the element neodymium (Nd), which belongs to the rare earths, iron and boron. Due to their extreme strength, neodymium magnets are used in many areas, for example in asynchronous generators of wind turbines or in the drives of electric cars.

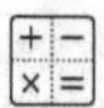

Excursus: Magnetising materials

You may know that you can magnetise certain non-magnetic metals with the help of a permanent magnet. If you rub the metal several times with a permanent magnet, it gradually becomes slightly magnetic. This is because the permanent magnet aligns the elementary magnets in the metal in one direction. Over time, the elementary magnets arrange themselves and remain in their position. A north and south pole is created - the metal is magnetised.

6.12. Displaying magnetic fields

Just as with the electric field, the magnetic field is represented by **field lines.**

! Magnetic field lines are always self-contained. They therefore do **not have a** starting and end point.

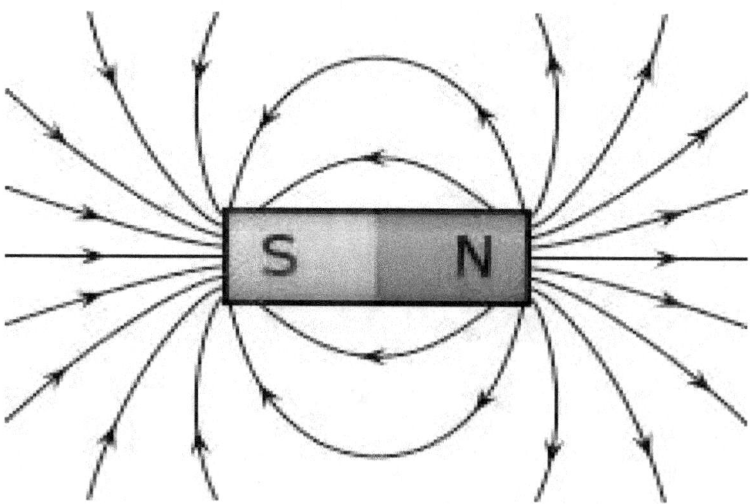

Figure 50: Magnetic field lines of a permanent magnet

The illustration shows magnetic lines of a permanent magnet. But these are not self-contained, are they?

Yes, they are closed, because the magnetic field lines continue **inside the magnet** from the south to the north pole, so that a closed circle is formed. We are only

Electrical engineering - current, voltage and co

interested in the **outer** field lines, which is why only these are drawn in many illustrations.

We can draw the magnetic field lines as an arrow from one pole to the other, knowing that the field lines continue inside the magnet. For the outer magnetic field lines it is then true that the starting point is always the north pole and the end point the south pole.

 As a mnemonic for drawing the field lines, it helps to say: "From north the arrow goes away".

As in any field, the **density of the magnetic field lines indicates the** strength of the magnetic field and is therefore a measure of the flux density $\vec{B}$.

A B-field is distributed **three-dimensionally** in space. When drawing, a convention has become established. A magnetic field that points into the drawing plane is marked by a cross. If it points out of the drawing plane, it is marked by a dot.

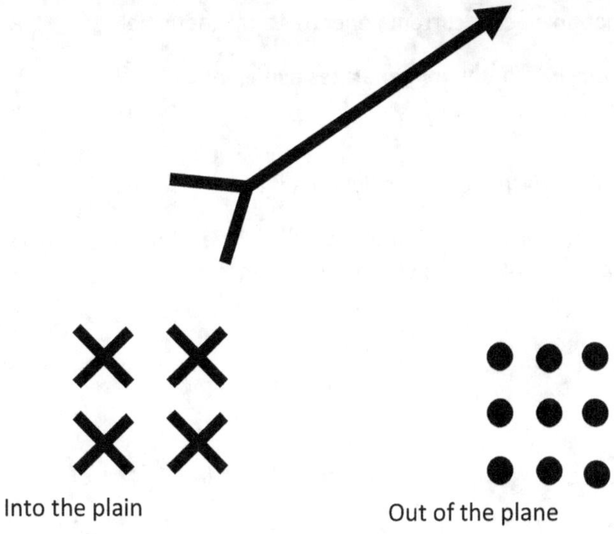

Figure 51: Representation of field lines

You can remember this definition by a feathered arrow. If you shoot the arrow into the plane, you see the tail, which is a two-dimensional cross. If the arrow flies towards us, we only see the tip, i.e. a point.

6.13. Electromagnetism

Static magnetic fields, such as that of a permanent magnet, are clear and familiar. Much more complex to understand are magnetic fields generated by electricity, for example in an electric motor.

Electromagnetism is one of the most important effects in our time and can be found almost everywhere. Electromagnetism plays a role in the electric car, in data transmission, in the high-voltage transmission of our power grid and in every power supply unit of a PC, laptop or smartphone.

To understand the effect, let's go back in time. In 1820, the physicist **Hans Christian Ørsted** experimented with a piece of wire through which he let current flow. In the process, he noticed that a compass located nearby deflected each time the voltage was applied. The magnetic needle no longer pointed north, but was **deflected by the wire through which current was flowing.** This finding quickly made the rounds and other physicists such as Ampère, after whom the current bar was named, were able to confirm the experiment.

This proved that an electric current generates a magnetic field.

 **A current-carrying conductor generates a magnetic field.**

But how do the field lines of the magnetic field run?

After some experiments, it was found that the resulting B-field builds up **concentrically around the conductor through which the current flows.**

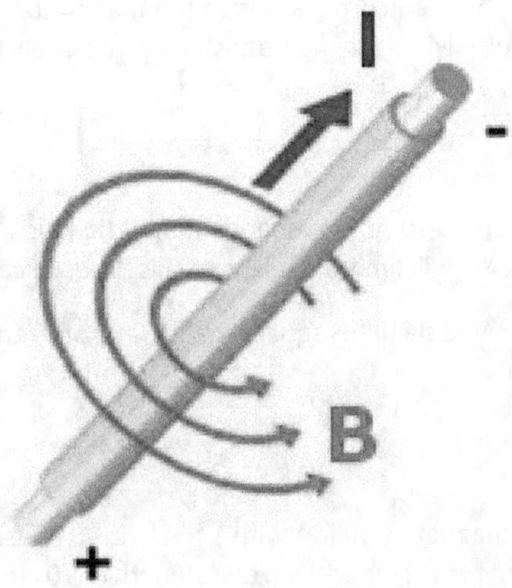

Figure 52: Magnetic field of a current-carrying conductor

The direction of the B-field can be determined with the **right-hand rule.** You clench a fist with your right hand and point your thumb upwards. This indicates the direction of flow of the current (in the technical direction of the current, i.e. from positive to negative pole). The four fingers indicate the direction of circulation of the B-field.

6.14. Induction law

In physics, most effects are valid **in both directions.** A current flow in the conductor generates a magnetic field. Conversely, an externally applied magnetic field generates a current flow in a conductor. This inversion is described as the **law of induction.** The process of **electromagnetic induction** means that a current or voltage is generated in a conductor by an external, changing magnetic field.

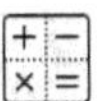

Derivation of induction

To do this, we will learn a new quantity. We already know the magnetic field and the magnetic flux density. The third significant quantity is the **magnetic flux Φ** (Greek letter capital Phi) will be dealt with.

The magnetic flux can be compared to a waterfall. We take a surface and hold it in the waterfall. We look at how much water flows through the surface.

The quantity that flows through the area corresponds to the magnetic flux. We obtain the magnetic flux by multiplying the flux density by the area flowed through.

$$\Phi = \vec{B} \cdot \vec{A}$$

 This relationship only applies to **homogeneous magnetic** fields, but in the context of this book we will limit ourselves to this "special case".

The unit of magnetic flux is given by Tesla times square metre Tm^2 or **Weber Wb** ($1\,\boldsymbol{Wb} = 1\,\boldsymbol{Tm^2}$).

We have a homogeneous magnetic field with the flux density of $B = 200\,mT$. We consider a square surface with an edge length of 10 cm. What is the magnetic flux?

Solution: $0.2\,T \cdot 0.1\,m \cdot 0.1\,m = 2\,mWb$

6.15. Magnetic flux and induction

The law of induction states that the voltage induced on a conductor depends on the **change in** magnetic flux over **time.** The temporal change is described by the differential (see 3.3.3)

$$U_{ind} = -\frac{d(B \cdot A)}{dt}$$

In practice, this means that a voltage is induced on a conductor when:

1. **the magnetic flux B changes over time**. This can be the case, for example, when more energy is supplied to an electromagnet and the field becomes larger as a result.

2. if the **area A** through which **the magnetic field passes changes.** This can be the case, for example, when the surface is pulled out of the B field or immersed.

The second effect is used, for example, in the dynamo known from bicycles: A permanent magnet rotates past a conductor. This causes the conductor to dip in

Electrical engineering - current, voltage and co

and out of the B-field with each rotation. According to the law of induction, a voltage is induced that operates the front and rear lights.

With the help of this system, a voltage can therefore also be induced from a movement. The law of induction is the basis for electro-mechanical systems such as electric motors and generators.

6.16. The Lenz Rule

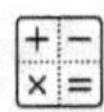

Nature is "lazy" and does not like to change. It strives for balance and homogeneity. This can be observed in many natural effects.

In electrical engineering there is an effect described by **Lenz's rule.** It states that the induced **voltage counteracts its cause** (the change in the B-field or area).

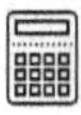

We explain this with an example.

- A conductor is **completely** in a B-field.

Since the B-field **does not change** and the conductor lies completely in the B-field, **no voltage** is induced. Let us now assume that the external magnetic field decreases due to external influences.

- The change in the magnetic field is **no longer zero.**

- **A voltage** is induced in the conductor.

- A current flows through the induced voltage.

- This **generates** a magnetic field that is **superimposed on the** external magnetic **field.**

- However, the magnetic field generated is polarised in such a way that it **counteracts the cause,** i.e. the decrease of the external B-field. Accordingly, it has a "building up instead of decreasing" effect.

-        The **generated magnetic field** "supports" the external magnetic field so that it decreases more slowly.

-        As a consequence of Lenz's rule, **no abrupt changes of the magnetic flux are possible.**

 The increase and decrease of the magnetic flux induces a voltage that counteracts the cause.

6.17. The Lorentz force

In the electric field, a sample charge Q experiences a **Coulomb force** that pulls the sample charge towards one pole and repels it from the other.

Similar to the electric field, test charges that are placed in the magnetic field experience a force. A test charge is not a charge particle, but a magnet. And as we have learned, a **current-carrying conductor** is also a magnet because it generates a magnetic field.

A force, the **Lorentz force,** acts on a **current-carrying** conductor in the magnetic field.

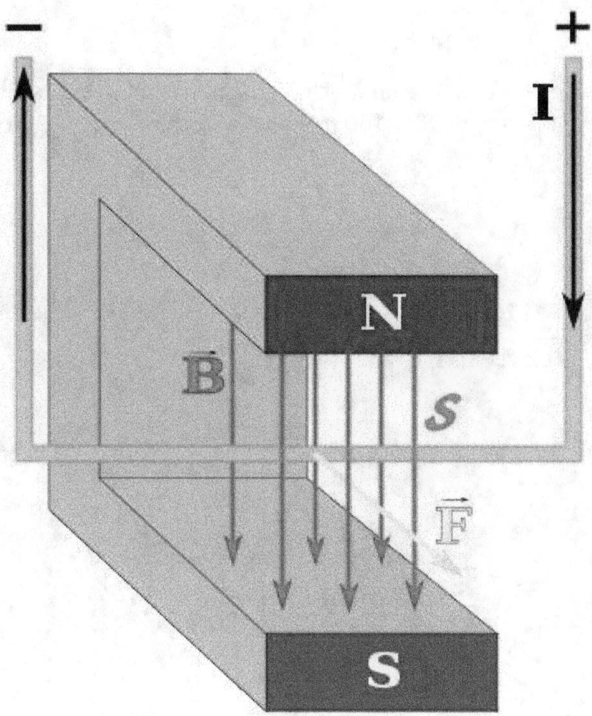

Figure 53: Lorentz force in the horseshoe magnet

As an example, we will use a **horseshoe magnet.** The advantage of this magnet is that the field within the legs of the horseshoe can be considered **approximately homogeneous.**

The B field flows from the north pole to the south pole. If we place a current-carrying piece of wire in the homogeneous magnetic field, it experiences a force. The magnitude of the force depends on the strength of the B field B the strength of the current I and the length s of the piece of wire.

$$F_L = I \cdot B \cdot s$$

What force is experienced by a conductor with a length of 10cm, through which 10 A flows and which is in a B field with a flux density of 200 mT?

Solution: $F_L = 10\ A \cdot 0.2T \cdot 0.1\ m = 0.2\ N$

What is the length s of a wire on which 7 *Millinewton* force acts on it when it is in a B-field of strength $B = 100\,mT$ and a current of $I = 200\,mA$ flowing through it?

Solution:

$$F_L = I \cdot B \cdot s$$

$$s = \frac{F_L}{I \cdot B} = \frac{7\,mN}{0.2\,A \cdot 0.1\,T} = 35\,cm$$

6.18. The direction of the Lorentz force, the three-finger rule

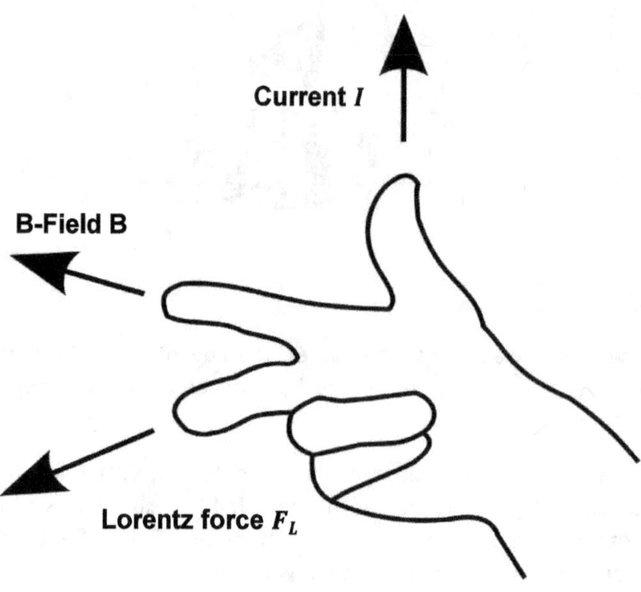

Figure 54: Three-finger rule

The direction of the force can be determined with the right-hand or three-finger rule. The **thumb, index finger and middle finger are** stretched out to form a **right-handed coordinate system** (right-hand system). The thumb is the direction of the technical current, the index finger is the direction of the magnetic field and the middle finger indicates the direction of the resulting force.

6.19. Overview: E-field and B-field

Finally, the following table illustrates all analogies of the electric and magnetic field. Strictly speaking, the Lorentz force is not a purely magnetic force effect, since a current-carrying conductor is necessary.

Type	E-field	B-field
Field strength	E	B
Field lines vividly		
Field constant	$\varepsilon_0 = 8.854 \cdot 10^{-12} \dfrac{As}{Vm}$	$\mu_0 = 1.257 \cdot 10^{-6} \dfrac{Vs}{Am}$
Cause	Charged bodies	Permanent magnets or current-carrying conductors
Test specimen	Test loading	Sample magnet/ current-carrying conductor
Field lines	Line along which a specimen experiences a force	
Field line orientation	From positive to negative pole	Closed, outside from north to south pole
Force effect	Coulomb force	Lorentz force
	$F_{el} = E \cdot q$	$F_L = I \cdot B \cdot s$

7. Mechanical and electromagnetic waves

After understanding both oscillations and the basics of electrical engineering, we come to the emission of electromagnetic waves.

Every type of wireless transmission is realised by electromagnetic waves. No matter whether it is the W-LAN from home, the mobile network or GPS of the mobile phone or the radio in the car radio.

The basis of electromagnetic waves is the electromagnetism already described. Electrons move back and forth and generate a **sinusoidal alternating current.** This means that the plus and minus poles change periodically. We refer to this movement as a **wave**.

7.1. Properties of waves

First of all, we do not limit ourselves to electromagnetic waves. There are numerous others, for example sound waves or water waves.

 In contrast to a vibration, a wave is not bound to a place, but spreads out in space.

Nevertheless, there are many analogies between vibrations and waves. But what is a wave actually?

The most illustrative is a water wave. We imagine a calm lake with a smooth water surface. There is no wave to be seen. But if we throw a stone into the lake, a wave spreads out in all directions around the stone's entry point.

A wave is a spreading disturbance. Usually the wave has a specific cause. In our example, this is the stone. By hitting the water surface, part of the kinetic energy is transferred to the water surface, which carries the additional energy away as a wave.

A wave transmits energy, but not matter. This is another difference between a wave and an oscillation. In an oscillation, the energy supplied is stored in different ways. For example, in spring and kinetic energy. A wave, on the other hand, transports the energy away, so the energy spreads out in space.

 A wave is an oscillation that propagates spatially. The particles that oscillate within a wave have **no** average speed of propagation in time.

We distinguish between two types of waves. *Longitudinal waves* and *transversal waves.*

With a longitudinal wave, the amplitude of the wave occurs in the direction of propagation. Colloquially, one also speaks of pressure or sound waves. This is because the propagation of sound is the prime example of a longitudinal wave.

Longitudinal waves

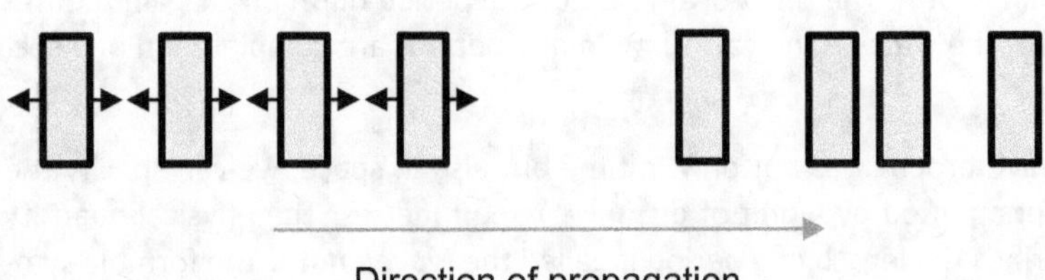

Figure 55: Representation of longitudinal waves

With transverse waves, on the other hand, the displacement takes place perpendicular to the direction of propagation of the wave. For example, with water waves or, as we will see later, with electromagnetic waves.

Transverse waves

Figure 56: Display of transverse waves

In practice, transverse waves occur much more frequently than longitudinal waves. A distinction is often made between mechanical waves and non-mechanical waves. Mechanical waves have vibrating particles that are coupled to each other.

In contrast, light waves, for example, also propagate in a vacuum, i.e. without carrier materials.

All equations that we will get to know can be used independently of the wave type.

We know by now what the difference is between an oscillation and a wave, but as always, we need concrete physical quantities and formulae to calculate.

Let's therefore look at some important physical quantities for describing waves.

As with an oscillation, a period duration can be assigned to a wave. This is the time in which a complete period is passed through. We designate the period duration again with T. The reciprocal value of the period duration is again the frequency f of the wave. It indicates how many periods are completed in one second.

Since a wave propagates not only in time but also in space, we can specify the distance of a period by a unit of distance, e.g. in metres. The physical quantity that describes the length of a period is called the **wavelength.** The formula symbol of the wavelength is λ (lambda).

We can always represent a wave in a location-dependent or **time-dependent way.**

As an example, we use a water wave. We can display the wave over the entire water surface and get the typical wave pattern.

Figure 57: Water wave after stone throwing

Spatial distribution of the amplitude at a **fixed point in time:**

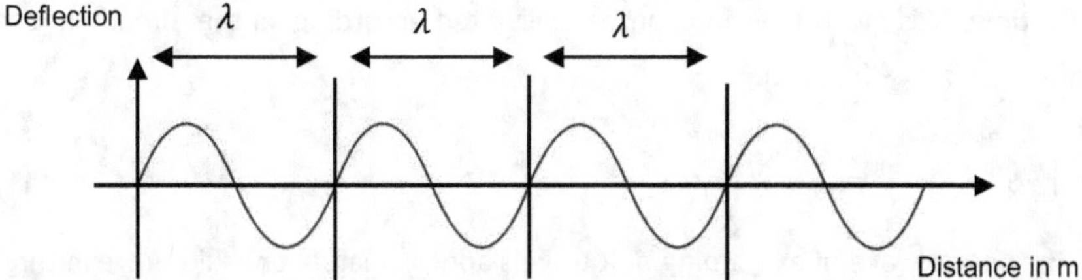

Figure 58: Propagation of the wave in space

On the other hand, we can observe a point on the water surface. At this point, the water rises and falls every time a wave passes. The displacement is time-dependent.

Time course of the amplitude at a **fixed point in** space:

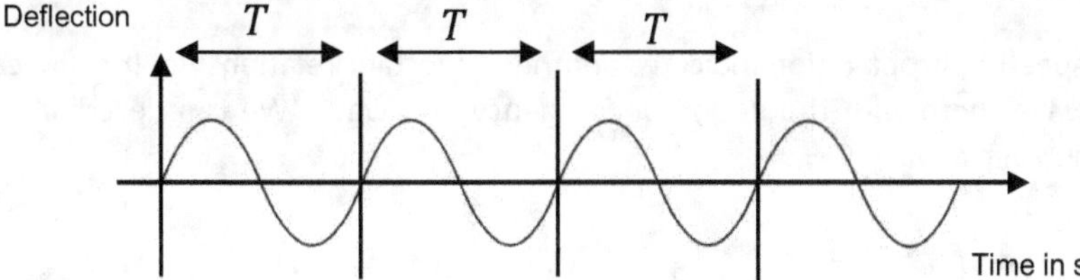

Figure 59: Temporal propagation of the wave at one point

Which points in space have the same displacement at any point in time?

Solution: The points that are exactly one wavelength apart.

As the last characteristic quantity of a wave, we need to know how fast it propagates in space. This quantity is described by the **speed of propagation $\vec{v}$ often also** called **c**. It is often also called the phase velocity of the wave.

We recognise that the velocity v is present as a vector, since it indicates a spatial direction, namely the direction of propagation of the wave. In the simplified case, the vector arrow is often omitted because it is clear from the context in which direction the wave is propagating, or because the wave propagates equally in all directions considered.

The speed of propagation forms the bridge of spatial propagation as a function of time. It is given in $\frac{m}{s}$ and can be calculated according to the already known formula $\vec{v} = \frac{s}{t}$ formula.

The sound wave of a lightning bolt travels approximately one kilometre in three seconds.

9 seconds after the lightning has struck in the distance, we hear the thunder of the lightning. What is the propagation speed of the thunder and how far away is the lightning?

Solution: $v = \frac{s}{t} = \frac{1000\,m}{3\,s} = 333.3\,\frac{m}{s}$

$$s = v \cdot t = 333.33\,\frac{m}{s} \cdot 9\,s = 3\,km$$

The speed of propagation indicates another important relationship. It connects the wavelength with the period or frequency of a wave. We can describe the relationship as

$$v = \frac{\lambda}{T} = \lambda \cdot f$$

If we know how fast a wave propagates and how long the wavelength is, we can determine the period and frequency.

$$T = \frac{\lambda}{v}\,;\ f = \frac{v}{\lambda}$$

If we know how fast a wave propagates and what the period or frequency is, we can determine the wavelength.

$$\lambda = v \cdot T = \frac{v}{f}$$

Why can't we hear anything in a vacuum, e.g. in space?

Solution:

Because sound needs a carrier matter, for example air molecules. There is almost no matter in space.

7.2. The Doppler effect

We have already learned about the propagation speed of waves. What happens when we send out the waves on a moving object? A classic example from everyday life is the siren of a police or ambulance car. The car is moving at a speed $\vec{v}_{car}$. In its normal state, the sound of the siren has a propagation speed of approx. $\vec{v}_{sound} = 340 \, \frac{m}{s}$. What happens when the moving vehicle emits sound waves?

Mathematically speaking, the velocity vectors of the sound and the car add or subtract each other. Explained graphically, the car travels behind the sound waves, causing the distances between the waves in front of the car to decrease and behind the car to increase. What physical quantity indicates how far apart two sound waves are? Exactly, the wavelength λ or, converted, the frequency f.

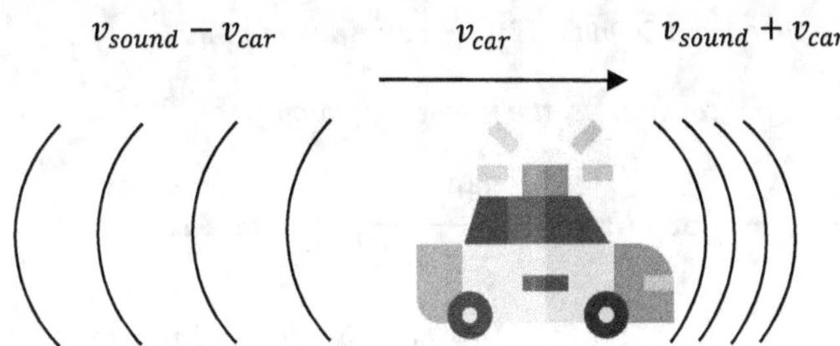

Figure 60: Doppler effect

As a result, the frequency increases when the sound source moves towards us and decreases when the sound source moves away from us. We can see exactly this effect in the siren of the police car. When the car passes us, the sound changes.

We can calculate the change in frequency if we know the speed of propagation of the wave and the speed of the vehicle. The new frequency f' is derived from the original frequency f as follows:

$$f' = f \cdot \frac{v_{sound}}{v_{sound} - v_{car}} \quad \text{When the vehicle is moving towards us}$$

$$f' = f \cdot \frac{v_{sound}}{v_{sound} + v_{car}} \quad \text{when the vehicle moves away from us.}$$

The effect of frequency shifting in moving objects was discovered by the astronomer Christian Doppler, after whom the **Doppler effect** was named. Nowadays, the frequency shift is also used to measure speeds in road traffic (radar traps).

A patrol car is on a chase and races the suspect with $v_{Police} = 120 \frac{km}{h}$ after the suspect. As it does so, the siren sounds, the sound waves of which propagate at the speed of sound. $v_{sound} = 340 \frac{m}{s}$ of sound. The sound of the siren has an original frequency of $f = 630\ Hz$.

At what frequency do we perceive the sound when the police car approaches us, when it just passes us and when it moves away from us again?

Solution:

First, we convert the speed into SI units. $120 \frac{km}{h}$ *correspond to* $33.3 \frac{m}{s}$

When the police car comes towards us, the frequency changes to:

$$f' = f \cdot \frac{v_{Sound}}{v_{Soundl} - v_{Police}} = 630\ Hz \cdot \frac{340 \frac{m}{s}}{340 \frac{m}{s} - 33.3 \frac{m}{s}} = 698.4\ Hz$$

When the police car passes us, the relative speed is zero and the sound is **630 Hz**.

When the police car moves away from us, the frequency changes to:

$$f' = f \cdot \frac{v_{Sound}}{v_{Sound} + v_{Police}} = 630\ Hz \cdot \frac{340 \frac{m}{s}}{340 \frac{m}{s} + 3.3 \frac{m}{s}} = 573.8\ Hz$$

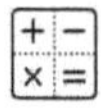

Another phenomenon occurs with jets, for example. A jet emits engine noise and air friction noise. We can hear it clearly on the ground. When a jet accelerates and gets faster and faster, it accumulates the sound waves in front of it. As the speed increases, the waves become denser and denser.

At the point where the jet has reached the speed of sound, the sound waves are all superimposed on a plane in front of the jet. The amplitude or volume of the waves adds up and a loud bang results - the sonic **boom**! The jet then moves

Mechanical and electromagnetic waves

faster than the sound. For passengers, the sounds emitted by the jet are no longer perceptible.

This concludes our excursion into sound waves and the Doppler effect. Next, we look at a class of waves that propagate much faster than the speed of sound.

7.3. Electromagnetic waves

After learning about the basic properties of waves and the Doppler effect, we move away from mechanical waves to waves that do not need a medium to propagate. We do not deal in detail with the generation of electromagnetic waves by means of antennas and oscillating circuits, but focus on physical properties and their use.

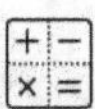

An electromagnetic wave is created by the interaction of electric and magnetic fields. As soon as a current is made to oscillate, it generates a changing electric field. We have learned that a current also produces a magnetic field at the same time.

At low frequencies, the electrons oscillate back and forth in the form of a measurable voltage and current in the conductors or cables.
However, if we increase the frequency at which the electrons oscillate back and forth, and dimension a suitable antenna, the oscillation can detach from the conductive paths into space. The wave is **radiated into** space. The frequencies of the waves must be selected extremely high.

When the wave is radiated from the conductor, the oscillating electrons remain in the conductor, because a wave does not transport matter. Only the electrical energy is converted into radiant energy by the wave and radiated.

The electric and magnetic fields are spatially shifted by 90° and are in turn 90° to the propagation speed.

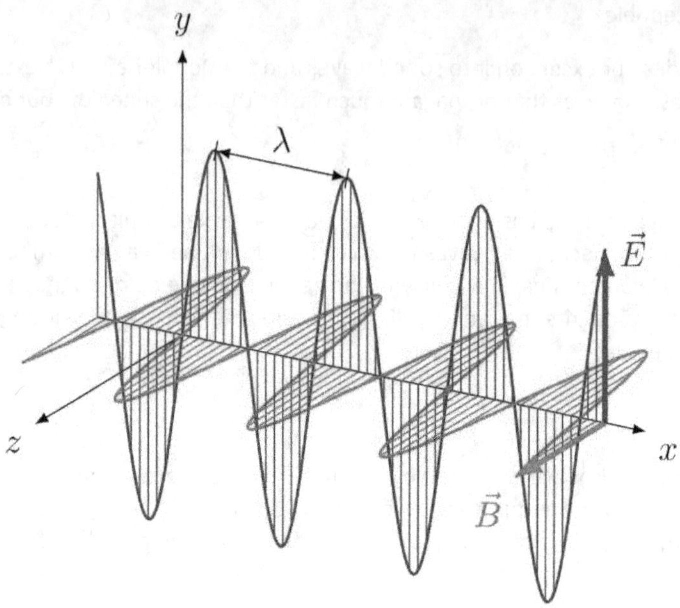

Figure 61: Electromagnetic wave

It has already been mentioned that the frequency of the oscillation must be very high so that the wave propagates. The following table helps us to get a feel for the magnitudes of different waves. Since the waves are classified according to their frequencies, we also speak of a (frequency) spectrum.

Designation	Wave frequency	Example
Low frequency	0 Hz to 50 Hz	---
	50 Hz	European electricity grid (conductor-based)
	Up to 30 kHz	Submarine communication
High frequency	Up to 3 MHz	Shortwave radio
	Up to 300 MHz	Radio and TV
	Up to 1 GHz	Mobile radio
	2.4 GHz	2.4-WLAN
	Up to 5 GHz	Bluetooth, 5G, GPS
	Up to 80 GHz	Radar
Infrared	> 300 GHz	Microwaves
(heat radiation)		Radiant heater
Light	> 300 THz	Visible light
UV rays	> 800 THz	Black light, photolithography
X-rays	> 30,000 THz	Medical technology

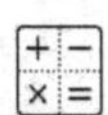

The European power grid is operated at a very low frequency of 50 Hz. This is because it is a wired oscillation, which is **not** supposed to detach. Every electromagnetic wave that detaches from the cables means a loss of energy during transport.

We have an overview of electromagnetic waves and their frequency. Next, we will look at the speed at which waves propagate in space.

7.4. The speed of light c

The speed of propagation of an electromagnetic wave in a vacuum can be derived from the natural constants of the electric and magnetic fields.

From the electric field constant ε_0 and the magnetic field constant μ_0 the speed of propagation of each electromagnetic wave is given by

$$v = \frac{1}{\sqrt{\varepsilon_0 \cdot \mu_0}}$$

We set the numerical values for ε_0 and μ_0 we get a speed of

$$v = \frac{1}{\sqrt{8.854 \cdot 10^{-12} \frac{As}{Vm} \cdot 1.257 \cdot 10^{-6} \frac{N}{A^2}}} = 299{,}792{,}458 \, \frac{m}{s} = c_0$$

The speed of propagation of an electromagnetic wave in a vacuum is called the **speed of light** and is expressed by the constant c or c_0 abbreviated. The speed of light is a fundamental natural constant that also plays a major role in other areas of physics.

The speed of light is often rounded for calculations. Instead of the exact numerical value of $299{,}792{,}458 \ \frac{m}{s}$ a speed of light of $300{,}000{,}000 \ \frac{m}{s} = 3 \cdot 10^8 \ \frac{m}{s}$ is used. This value is easier to remember, it is simple to enter into the calculator or computer and corresponds to the numerical value with an accuracy of 99.993%. For calculations, we therefore henceforth use the value $c = 3 \cdot 10^8 \ \frac{m}{s}$.

The propagation speed of an electromagnetic wave in other media depends on the respective material constants ε_r and μ_r.

Since air has a dielectric constant ε_r and a permeability μ_r of almost unity, the propagation speed in air is only 0.28% lower than in a vacuum. We can therefore use the speed of light as the propagation speed of electromagnetic waves in air as a good approximation.

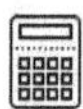

The radio station "Antenne Bayern" broadcasts at a frequency of approximately 100 MHz. What is the propagation speed of the wave? What is the wavelength of the wave?

Solution:
The speed of propagation of the wave corresponds to the speed of light $c = 3 \cdot 10^8 \frac{m}{s}$.

The wavelength is calculated as

$$\lambda = \frac{v}{f} = \frac{c}{f} = \frac{3 \cdot 10^8 \ \frac{m}{s}}{100 \cdot 10^6 \ Hz} = 3 \ m$$

What is the wavelength of the WLAN network? (We can find the frequency in the table above).

Solution:

$$\lambda = \frac{c}{f} = \frac{3 \cdot 10^8 \ \frac{m}{s}}{2.4 \ Ghz} = \frac{3 \cdot 10^8 \ \frac{m}{s}}{2.4 \cdot 10^9 \ Hz} = 0.25 \ m = 12.5 \ cm$$

Mechanical and electromagnetic waves

In water, the propagation speed of light is about 25% lower than in air or in a vacuum. How long is a wavelength of WLAN signals there?

Solution:

$$\lambda = \frac{75\% \cdot c}{f} = \frac{0.75 \cdot 3 \cdot 10^8 \frac{m}{s}}{2.4\ Ghz} = \frac{2.25 \cdot 10^8 \frac{m}{s}}{2.4 \cdot 10^9\ Hz} = 0.094\ m = 9.4\ cm$$

We have dealt with the essential properties of mechanical and electromagnetic waves. In this context, we have already learned about the speed of light without going into more detail about what light is in the first place. Because light is much more extensive than you would initially think.

8. Optics - light and refraction

For most of the history of our existence, the daily routine of humans had to follow a natural phenomenon, the day-night rhythm. With a few exceptions, work could only be done during the day.

The invention of an artificial light source in the form of an incandescent lamp in 1835 decoupled working hours from the day-night rhythm.

Today's LCD displays and LED spotlights allow us to work in front of the PC at night or enjoy football matches in floodlights.

But what is this light that determines our entire everyday life?

8.1. Light - an electromagnetic wave

Light is electromagnetic radiation, just like WLAN, GPS or Bluetooth. The frequencies are in the terrahertz range. That is why we more often speak of wavelengths and not frequencies in connection with light. We can convert the two quantities into each other at any time using the well-known constant of the speed of light. Each colour has a characteristic wavelength.

The human eye can only recognise a certain part of the spectrum. This part of the spectrum is therefore also called *visible light.*

Frequency spectrum					
Frequency	$10^{17}\ Hz$ $-\ 10^{20}\ Hz$	$10^{15}\ Hz$ bis $-\ 10^{17}\ Hz$	$4,3 \cdot 10^{14}\ Hz$ $-7,5 \cdot 10^{14}\ Hz$	$10^{12}\ Hz$ $-\ 10^{14}\ Hz$	$300\ Hz$ $-\ 300\ M$
Wave length	$1\ nm$	$100\ nm$	$380\ nm$ bis $780\ nm$	$1\ \mu m - 1\ cm$	$1\ m - 1$

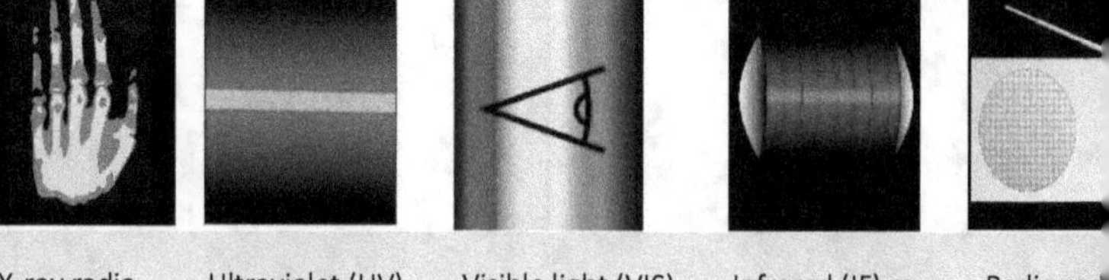

X-ray radiation	Ultraviolet (UV) radiation	Visible light (VIS)	Infrared (IF) radiation	Radio radiation

Figure 62: Frequency spectrum

Within visible light, we find different colours at different frequencies.

The colours blue and red are at the edge of visible light at a wavelength of $\lambda_{Blue} \approx 470\ nm$ and $\lambda_{Red} \approx 700\ nm$ Green, yellow and orange tones are in the middle of visible light.

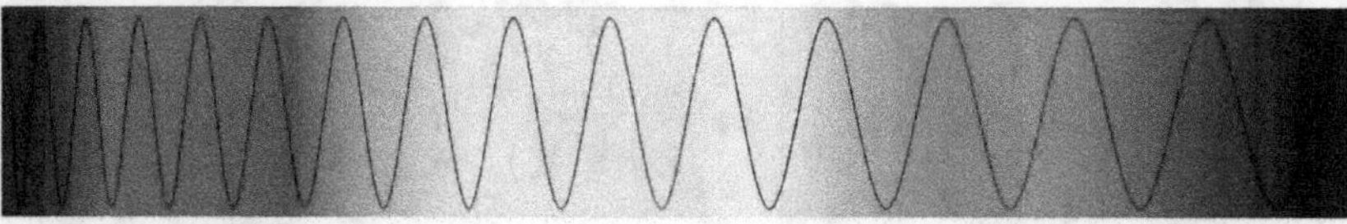

Figure 63: Spectrum of visible light

Colour version of the book in better resolution as a free eBook - See at the end of the book!

However, the light of the sun also contains ultraviolet and infrared components that we cannot perceive. We must always keep in mind that it is only due to our eyes that we can see this part of the spectrum. Our eye is nothing more than a biological sensor that can only pick up these specific waves. Animals such as fish or bees, on the other hand, can also "see" into the UV range.

We have clarified the physical meaning of light as an electromagnetic wave. Building on this, we will look at two other effects that benefit spectacle wearers in particular, the refraction and reflection of waves. These principles are not limited to light or electromagnetic waves, but we will focus on optics. First, we will look at the phenomenon of **refraction.**

8.2. Refraction

Everyone knows the phenomenon as soon as you look at a water surface. Objects under the water surface seem much closer than they really are.

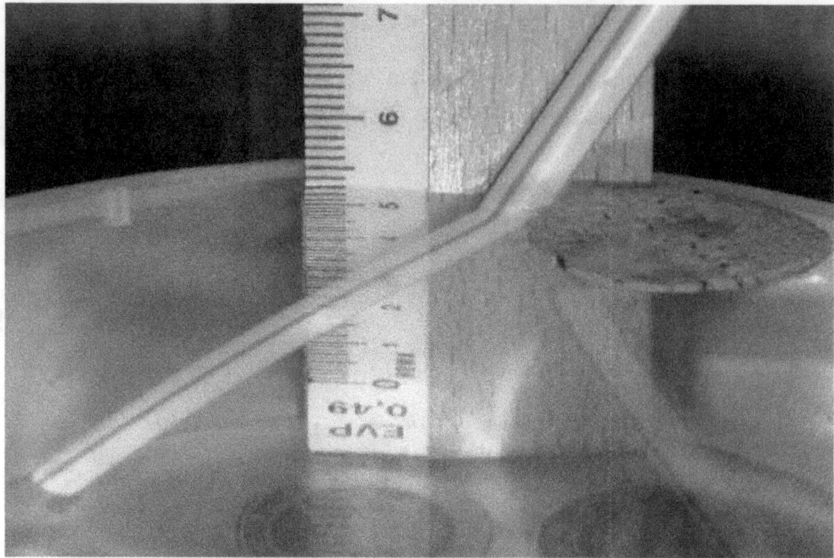

Figure 64: Refraction at the water surface

Refraction occurs during the transition from one medium (air) to another medium (water). The angle of the wave to the perpendicular of the transition surface changes.

The perpendicular is the vertical line through the breaking point or entry point of the wave into the water.

The reason for this is that the propagation speed of light depends on the medium. In water, the speed of propagation is not equal to the speed of light in air, but is reduced by about 25%.

This is illustrated by an example: On a busy beach, a man in the water calls for help. A lifeguard sees the man and has to rescue him as quickly as possible. The lifeguard can run much faster on land than he can swim in the water. Therefore, he will stay on land for as long as possible and only cover the necessary distance in the water.

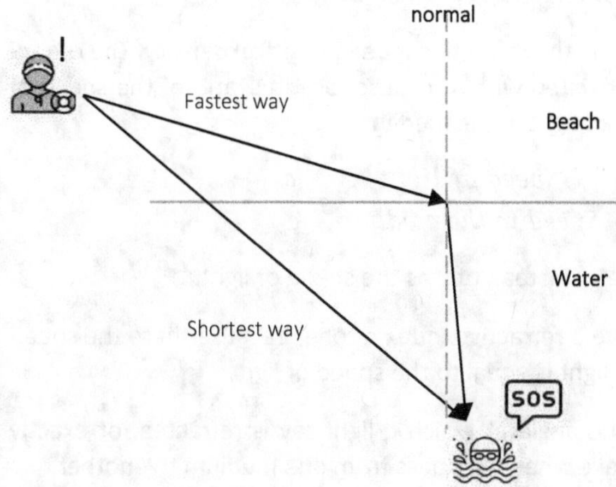

Figure 65: Analogy - Lifeguard

The lifeguard understandably chooses the quickest route, not the shortest.

A physical phenomenon discovered by the French physicist Pierre Fermat and named after him is very similar to the example with regards to the refractive behaviour of light.

Fermat's principle states that light, in order to travel from one point to another, always seeks the path of **minimum travel time** and not the shortest path. This is also the case, for example, with our initial example of the refraction of air in water.

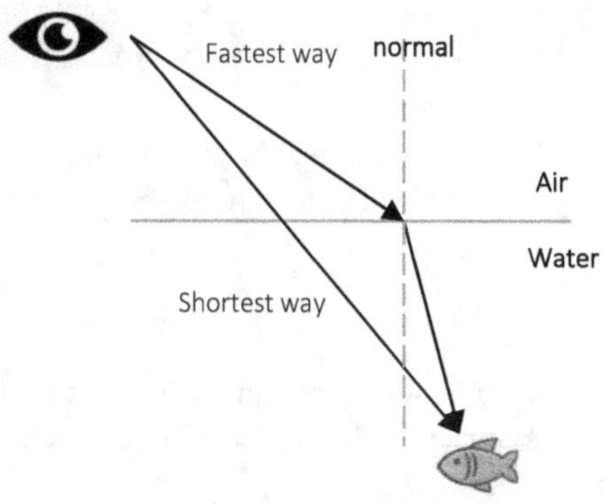

Figure 66: Difference between fastest and shortest route

In order to calculate refraction, we need a number that describes the properties of a material in relation to the speed of propagation.

This number is called the **refractive index** or **optical density.** The refractive index is abbreviated with n. It describes the ratio of the speed of light to the speed of light in the medium.

$$n = \frac{Speed\ of\ light}{Speed\ in\ the\ medium} = \frac{c_0}{c_M}$$

To avoid confusion, we use c_0 instead of c as the speed of light.

Air or vacuum have a refractive index of one, because there the speed of propagation of light is equal to the speed of light.

Next, we look at the angle at which a light ray is refracted, or exactly which path the light rays take when they pass from one medium to another.

This question can be solved mathematically by an extreme value problem. In physics, one calculates exclusively with the result.

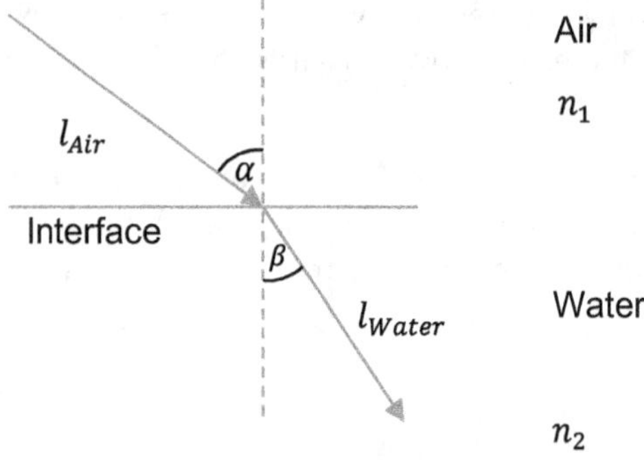

Figure 67: Refraction of air in water

The transit time of the light beam should become minimal. This condition is fulfilled if the product of the sine of the angle and the refractive index remains the same.

$$\sin(\alpha) \cdot n_1 = \sin(\beta) \cdot n_2$$

This law, which is based on Fermat's principle, was named Snell**'s law of refraction** after the Dutch mathematician Willebrord van Roijen **Snell.**

Let's apply the law of refraction to our water surface. The refractive index of air is 1, that of water is approximately

Optics - light and refraction

$n_{Water} = 1.3$. When a ray of light falls on the water surface at an angle of 60° to the perpendicular, it is refracted according to the law of refraction. We can calculate the resulting angle.

$$\sin(60) \cdot 1 = \sin(\beta) \cdot .3$$

$$\beta = \arcsin\left(\frac{\sin(60°)}{1.3}\right) = 41.8°$$

The angle is reduced from 60° to 41.6°. This refracts the beam towards the perpendicular.

 In a transition from one medium to another, light is refracted towards the perpendicular as the refractive index increases and away from the perpendicular as the refractive index decreases.

Material	Refractive index
Vacuum	1
Air	Nearly 1
Ice cream	1.3
Water	1.33
Glass	1.4 ... 2.2
Quartz glass	1.46
Benzene	1.5
Polycarbonate (PC)	1.585
Spectacle lenses (plastic)	Up to 1.76
Sulphur	2
Diamond	2.4

A beam of light is refracted by ice in air. Is it refracted towards the perpendicular or away?

The angle α is 20°, what is the exit angle β?

Solution:

The refractive index of ice is $n_1 = 1.3$, the refractive index of air is $n_2 = 1$. Since $n_2 < n_1$ the beam is broken away from the perpendicular

$$\sin(\alpha) \cdot n_1 = \sin(\beta) \cdot n_2$$

$$\sin(20°) \cdot 1.3 = \sin(\beta) \cdot 1$$

$$\beta = \arcsin(\frac{1.3 \cdot \sin(20°)}{1}) = 26.4°$$

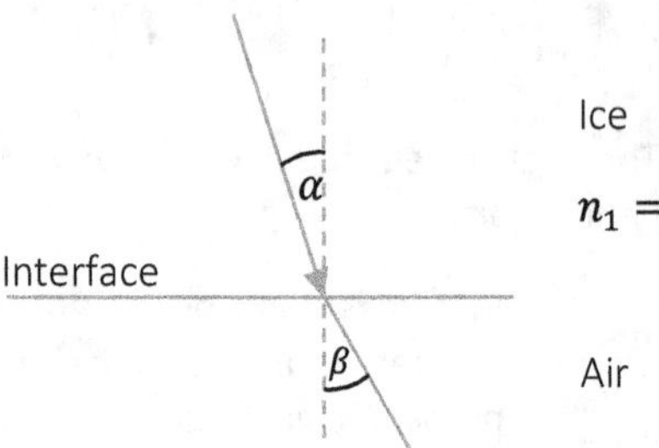

Figure 68: Example of refraction of ice in air

The refractive index of an unknown substance is determined by directing a laser pointer at an angle of $\alpha = 45°$ onto the substance. We observe an angle $\beta = 26.5°$. What material is it?

Solution:

$$\sin(\alpha) \cdot n_1 = \sin(\beta) \cdot n_2 \rightarrow \sin(45°) \cdot 1 = \sin(26.5°) \cdot n_2$$

$$n_2 = 1 \cdot \frac{\sin(45°)}{\sin(26.5°)} = 1{,}585$$

A comparison with the refractive indices in the table shows: The material is polycarbonate.

8.3. Reflection

When light waves change from one material to another, they are not only refracted but also partially reflected back. For example, the shore is reflected when we look at a lake. This effect is also called **reflection.**

The same laws apply as for refraction.

$$\sin(\alpha) \cdot n_1 = \sin(\beta) \cdot n_2$$

However, since the material does not change, the refractive indices are the same. Consequently, the angles are also the same.

$$\sin(\alpha) \cdot n_1 = \sin(\beta) \cdot n_2 \rightarrow \sin(\alpha) = \sin(\beta) \rightarrow \alpha = \beta$$

In reflection, the angle of incidence is equal to the angle of reflection. Refraction and reflection usually occur together, depending on the refractive indices.

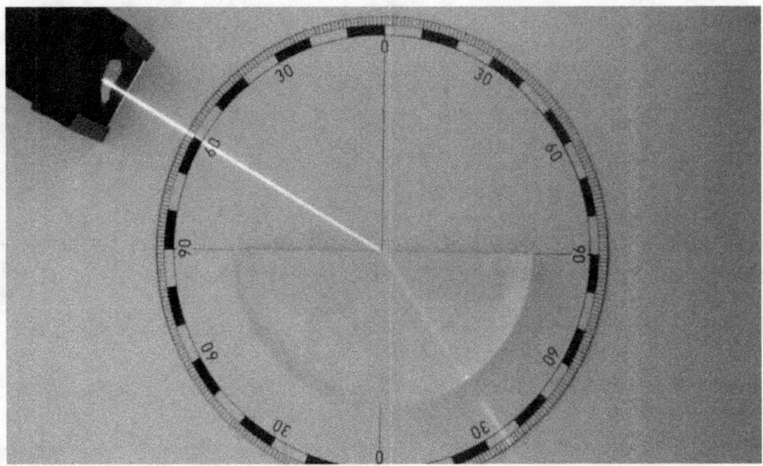

Figure 69: Partial reflection and partial refraction

8.4. Total reflection

In the case of total reflection, all the light is reflected back and not partially refracted. We can first logically deduce when this is the case. If a light beam enters a matter with a smaller refractive index, for example from glass into air, the beam is refracted away from the perpendicular. What happens if we keep increasing the angle of entry and thus also the angle of exit? At some point we reach a critical angle at which the exit angle becomes greater than 90°. From this angle on, the beam is no longer refracted but completely reflected. This is called **total reflection**.

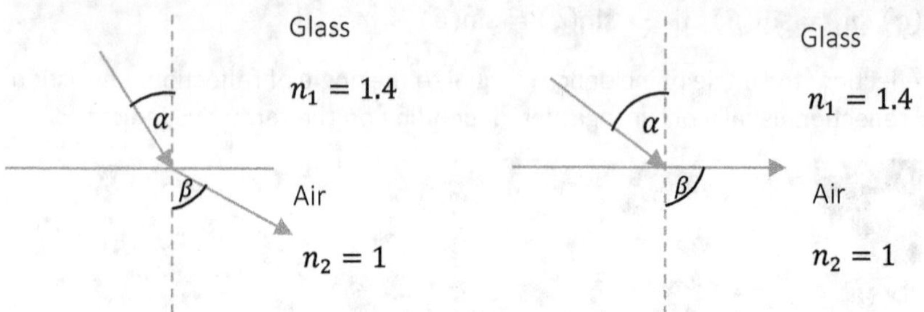

Figure 70: Boundary case in the refraction of glass to air

We can determine the critical angle at which total reflection occurs by the law of refraction. At the critical angle $\alpha_{critical}$ the angle β is exactly 90°.

This results in $\alpha_{critical}$ from:

$$\sin(\alpha_{critical}) \cdot n_1 = \sin(90°) \cdot n_2$$

$$\sin(\alpha_{critical}) \cdot n_1 = 1 \cdot n_2$$

$$\alpha_{critical} = arcsin\left(\frac{n_2}{n_1}\right)$$

For our example of glass to air, this results in a critical angle of

$$\alpha_{critical} = arcsin\left(\frac{1}{1.4}\right) = 45.6°.$$

From an angle of 45.6°, no more light rays are refracted.

8.5. Refraction through lenses

We can use the effect of refraction to deflect light rays in a way that is advantageous for a particular problem. For example, eyeglass lenses compensate for the biological inaccuracy of the eyeball.

An optically transparent disc with one or two curved sides is called a **lens.** If the surface is curved, usually parabolic, it is called a **convex** lens; otherwise it is called a **concave** lens.

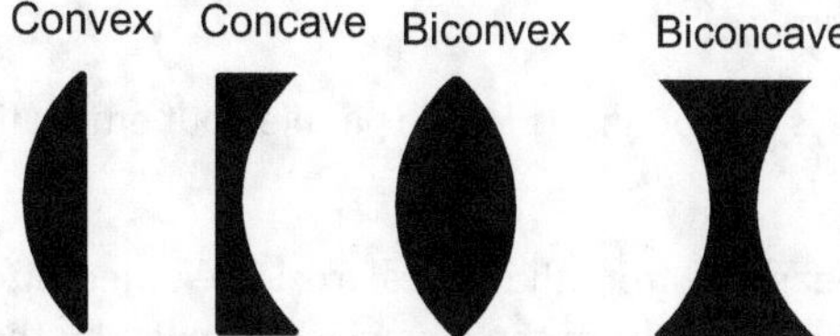

Figure 71: Different lens shapes

The task of a lens is to refract parallel incident light rays at the surface in order to focus (converging lens) or scatter (diverging lens) the light rays. A (bi-) convex lens focuses the light rays, a (bi-) concave lens scatters the light rays.

To illustrate the path of light rays through a lens, we place a horizontal axis and a vertical axis through the lens. The horizontal axis is called the **optical axis**, the vertical axis is called the lens **plane.**

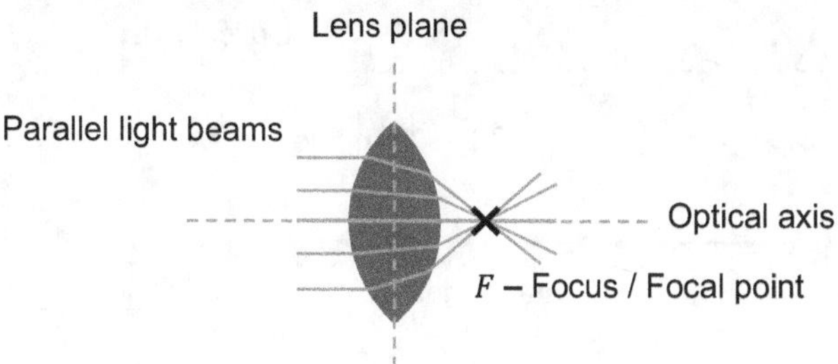

Figure 72: Beam path of a converging lens

The point at which a convex lens focuses all parallel rays of light is called the **focal point. The** distance of the focal point from the lens plane is called the **focal length.** f is called the focal length.

The focal length f of a lens is a characteristic property and can be determined by the curvature, material, thickness or surface properties of the lens.

A focal point is also defined for a concave lens, but this is not vivid, which is why we restrict ourselves to convex lenses, i.e. converging lenses.

Through this focusing effect, a fire can be created with the help of a simple magnifying glass or a convex lens by focusing the parallel rays of the sun into one point. The complete energy of the light rays is also concentrated there, so that there is enough energy to ignite a fire.

But what happens when the light rays do not hit the lens in parallel, but emanate from a point, for example an object?

The object has a height, which is measured from the optical axis. The object size is denoted by G. The distance of the object from the lens plane is given by the distance of the object from the lens plane with g.

The light rays from the object pass through the lens, are refracted and project an image behind the lens plane. The distance of the image from the lens plane is denoted by b and the height of the image is given by B.

The following figure illustrates the relationship between the quantities. In addition, refraction causes a reflection of the object on the optical axis.

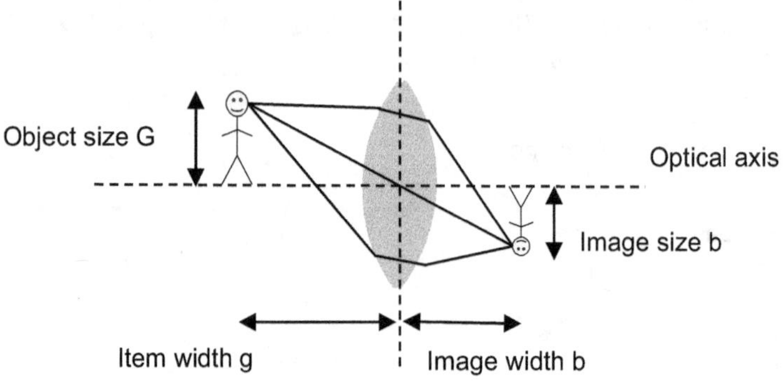

Figure 73: Image and object width of a converging lens

The larger the object, the larger the image will be at the same distance. If we move the object further away from the lens plane, the image also becomes smaller.

The ratio of image and object size is equal to the ratio of image and object width. The relatively simple equation is:

$$\frac{B}{G} = \frac{b}{g}$$

In addition, another relationship can be established, which is listed without mathematical proof. The so-called lens equation describes the relationship between object width, image width and focal length. We remember that the focal length is a property of the lens, which is independent of the respective image. The equation for determining the focal length is:

$$\frac{1}{f} = \frac{1}{g} + \frac{1}{b}$$

When specifying spectacle lenses, one usually does not use the focal length f but the **refractive power D** which is given in diopters $[D] = dpt$. A lens with a focal length of $f = 0.8\ m$ has a refractive power of $\frac{1}{f} = 1.25\ dpt$.

A tree which is $g = 100\ m$ from the lens plane is projected by a lens camera onto a white background at a distance of $b = 10\ cm$ projected.

The image of the tree on the screen is $B = 5\ m$ high. How high is the real tree? What is the focal length and refractive power of the lens?

Solution:
We use the lens refraction law:

$$\frac{B}{G} = \frac{b}{g} \rightarrow G = \frac{g}{b}B \rightarrow G = \frac{100\ m}{10\ cm} \cdot 5\ cm = 50\ m$$

$$\frac{1}{f} = \frac{1}{g} + \frac{1}{b} \rightarrow f = \frac{1}{\frac{1}{g} + \frac{1}{b}} = \frac{1}{\frac{1}{100\ m} + \frac{1}{10\ cm}} \approx 9.999\ cm$$

$$\frac{1}{f} = \frac{1}{9.999\ cm} = 10.01\ dpt$$

In this chapter, we have always considered light as an electromagnetic wave. Another theory sees light as a stream of particles and not as a wave. Here, so-called photons are the carriers of energy. In this theory, a beam of light consists of countless photons that are emitted. A photon is the smallest possible light particle.

But which theory is correct? Are photons particles with a mass or an electromagnetic wave? The truth is that both models are correct. We have learned that a model should only represent as good a representation of reality as possible so that we can apply mathematical operations. Light shows properties that we can apply to both theories, for example, it can be refracted and thus has wave character. However, we can now also look at individual photons, which speaks for the particle character.

Since the introduction of quantum theory, it has been clear that light particles exhibit the properties of both classical particles and classical waves.

 We can refract and deflect light. On the other hand, we can shoot individual photons at each other and bounce them off of each other like classical particles. This fact is also described as **wave-particle duality.**

Wave-particle duality is not limited to light, but also to other particles such as electrons.

9. Nuclear physics

In this chapter we look at the most important aspects of nuclear physics. How much does an electron weigh? What is radioactivity and what are the different types of radiation?

We have already learned about the structure of an atom.

In the atomic nucleus, neutrons and protons are crowded together in a very small space. Electrons race around the nucleus in different orbits, also called shells. Overall, the atom is neutrally charged, which means that we can find as many electrons as protons in an atom.

We have already learned about the charge of electrons, which we call the elementary charge $e = 1.602 \cdot 10^{-19}$ C

However, we have not yet determined the mass of an electron in more detail. Electrons, like light, can be regarded both as particles with a mass and as waves.

The mass of an electron is another natural constant and is vanishingly small. It amounts to $m_e = 9.11 \cdot 10^{-31}$ kg. Protons and neutrons, on the other hand, are about 1800 times heavier with a mass of $m_p = 1.67 \cdot 10^{-27}$ kg.

Next, we deal with different atoms, from hydrogen to uranium or plutonium.

In the process, individual sections become blurred with other subject areas. Atomic numbers and the mass of atoms are also basic principles of chemistry. A clear separation is therefore not possible.

9.1. The atomic number Z

The atomic number of an atom indicates the number of its protons and electrons.

The **atomic number Z** determines the atom. It indicates the number of protons in the atomic nucleus and the number of electrons around the nucleus.

The mass of an atom depends largely on the number of protons and neutrons. These are called nucleons. The number of neutrons in an atom is also called the neutron number N.

The sum of protons and neutrons is also called the **mass number A**. $A = Z + N$

Theoretically, we have to add the electron mass to determine the mass of an atom. As we have already seen, however, this has hardly any influence.

The smallest and lightest element is hydrogen. It has the **atomic number one, which** means that it consists of only one proton and one electron. The mass number is also one, which means that it has no neutrons.

Iron, on the other hand, has the **atomic number 26** - it therefore consists of 26 protons. In addition, there are 30 neutrons in the nucleus. The mass number is correspondingly $A = 26 + 30 = 56$ so that the iron atom is about 56 times as large as the nucleus of a hydrogen atom.

To represent an atom, the abbreviation is first used, for example H for hydrogen (hydrogen) or Fe for iron (ferrite).

The mass number and the atomic number are written in front of it, $_Z^A Element$.

For hydrogen and iron, this would look like this:

$_1^1 H$ and $_{26}^{56} Fe$.

The mass number is often omitted if it is not necessary for the description. In the following chapter, however, it is essential to specify the mass number.

9.2. Isotopes

We have established that the atom is determined by the atomic number. Is every atom therefore exactly the same? Not necessarily. In the vast majority of cases a specific composition of atomic number and mass number dominates. Let's take the carbon atom as an example. It has the atomic number 6 and is abbreviated with C (carbon).

Most carbon atoms have an additional 6 neutrons in the nucleus. Thus we can describe it as $_6^{12} C$. As always in nature, there are also exceptions. For example, carbon atoms with 7 neutrons and thus 13 nucleons. Carbon atoms with 8 or more neutrons do not occur because they are too unstable due to their high mass and decay.

If an element occurs with different numbers of neutrons, these are called **isotopes.** They can occur in a stable state or in a temporary, unstable state.

In nature, the $^{12}_{6}C$ atom occurs with a probability of 98.9 %. Only 1.1% of the carbon atoms that occur are $^{13}_{6}C$ atoms.

If we want to calculate the mass of a carbon body, we have to calculate the mass of an average carbon atom. This is calculated from the arithmetic mean, where the occurrence probabilities are multiplied by the mass number.

$$A_{Durchscnitt} = 13 \cdot 1.1\,\% + 12 \cdot 98.9\,\% = 13 \cdot 0.011 + 12 \cdot 0.989 = \mathbf{12.011}$$

The average mass number of a carbon atom is 12.011. Therefore, the average carbon atom is often given as $^{12.011}_{6}C$ is given.

If an atomic isotope becomes too low in mass, the atomic nucleus or the whole atom may become unstable. It decays into smaller atoms and emits radioactive radiation.

9.3. Radioactive decay

When an atom changes from an unstable state to a stable state by emitting radioactive radiation, this is called radioactive decay. As disasters like Fukushima or Chernobyl show, uncontrolled radioactive decay can have devastating effects on animals and humans. The term radioactive decay goes back to the Polish chemist Marie Curie. For her research on radioactivity, she was awarded the Nobel Prize in Physics in 1903 and the Nobel Prize in Chemistry in 1911. Unfortunately, her years of research with radioactive elements proved to be her undoing, as she died of the health consequences in 1934.

However, there are different types of radioactive radiation. Some are relatively harmless and can be shielded with the help of a sheet of paper, other types of radiation penetrate house walls and metal plates. Therefore, we look at different types of radiation.

We begin with the type of radiation that was discovered first and is therefore simply abbreviated with the first letter of the Greek alphabet - alpha radiation.

9.4. Alpha radiation

With α**radiation, alpha particles** are emitted. Alpha particles consist of two protons and two neutrons. The atom that consists of exactly 2 protons and two neutrons and two electrons is called **helium.** $^{4}_{2}He.$

! The difference between alpha particles and helium is that alpha parti-
cles lack the two electrons. That is why we often speak of helium nuclei.

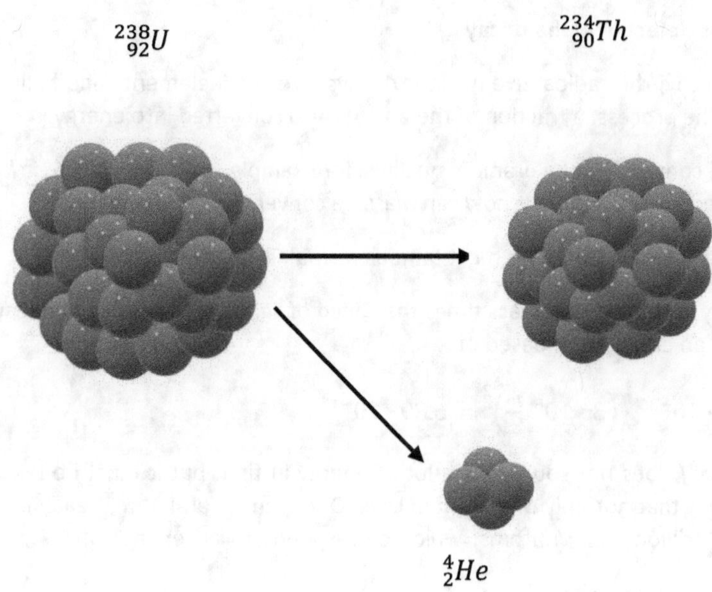

Figure 74: Decay of uranium

An example process for the release of alpha radiation is the radioactive substance uranium. Uranium has the atomic number 92 and the mass number 238,
$^{238}_{92}U$. It is radioactive and decays into smaller atoms by emitting alpha radiation
(helium nucleus), for example thorium with atomic number 90 and mass number
234.

$$^{238}_{92}U \rightarrow {}^{234}_{90}Th + {}^{4}_{2}He$$

Furthermore, additional energy is released in the form of heat during decay.

Since the alpha radiation is "missing" two **electrons**, it is **positively charged.**

Since alpha particles are helium nuclei, they can be captured or blocked with
almost any kind of matter. A sheet of paper is already sufficient to capture the
helium nuclei. Alpha radiation is therefore relatively harmless to humans. From
the outside, the radiation is already blocked by the uppermost layers of skin

without causing any far-reaching damage. It becomes dangerous when a radio-active substance enters the body and it can damage internal, healthy cells.

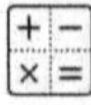

Mass defect in alpha decay

In alpha decay, the radioactive nucleus decays into small elements and helium nuclei. In the process, a fraction of the mass is also converted into energy.

During the conversion of a uranium nucleus, for example, a mass of $7 \cdot 66^{-30} kg$ is converted into energy. But how can mass be converted into energy?

This is where Albert Einstein's most famous formula comes in: $E = m \cdot c^2$.

The energy is equal to the mass times the speed of light squared. For our decay, therefore, an energy is released of

$$E = 7.66 \cdot 10^{-30} \cdot \left(3 \cdot 10^8 \ \tfrac{m}{s}\right)^2 = 6.89 \cdot 10^{-13} \ J.$$

$6.89 \cdot 10^{-13} J$ does not sound like a lot of energy at first, but it must be taken into account that not only one atom decays. One gram of uranium already contains 2.53 trillion (10^{21}) atoms, which corresponds to an energy of 1.7 giga joules!

9.5. Beta radiation

With **β radiation, beta particles** are emitted. Beta particles are produced when there is an unbalanced ratio of protons and neutrons in an atomic nucleus. If there are too few protons but too many neutrons, a neutron is converted into a proton to compensate. In the process, the excess charge is released as β radiation.

Since the charge released is negatively charged, it is also called β^- radiation. The charge particle is an electron e^- .

This is why we often speak of **beta-minus decay** and beta-minus **radiation** or beta-minus **particles.**

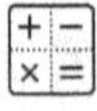

On the other hand, there may also be too few neutrons. Then a proton is converted into a neutron and a β^+ radiation is emitted. In the process, a positron e^+ is released. Positrons are less well known than electrons because they occur almost exclusively in beta decay and are not very illustrative. The process is called beta-plus decay.

If a neutron is converted into a proton, the mass number does not change, but the atomic number increases by one. Our carbon atom provides an example. In its nucleus, it consists of 6 protons and 6 neutrons ($^{12}_{6}C$) or 7 neutrons ($^{13}_{6}C$). We also know that it is stable with mass numbers 12 and 13.

If an additional neutron is added to the nucleus, we obtain $^{14}_{6}C$, an unstable element, which immediately converts a neutron into a proton. As the number of protons is increased, we get a new, stable element nitrogen $^{14}_{7}N$. Enormous energy is generated, which carries the newly created electrons out of the atom.

 When a neutron is converted into a proton, an electron is emitted as beta radiation.

$$^{14}_{6}C \rightarrow {}^{14}_{7}N + e^{-}$$

The energy of the released electrons depends on the material. Beta radiation is more difficult to shield than alpha radiation, but it is still relatively easy. An aluminium plate, which only needs to be a few millimetres thick, is sufficient.

The last type of radiation, on the other hand, is much more energetic and more difficult to shield. We are talking about gamma radiation.

9.6. Gamma radiation

The **γ radiation** usually occurs in combination with alpha or beta radiation when the atom still has excess energy after decay. This is emitted in the form of a high-energy electromagnetic wave. Gamma radiation is usually a side effect of alpha or beta decay. The gamma particles are also called **photons.**

The frequency of the electromagnetic wave is above all previously known waves with frequencies in the range of $f = 6 \cdot 10^{19}\ Hz$ or a wavelength of $\lambda = 5\ pm\ (Pikometer)$.

Gamma radiation is very energetic and because it is an electromagnetic wave, it can propagate through almost any element. The high energy can cause damage to cells or human DNA, which can trigger infertility, tumours or deformities. Attenuation is achieved by high-density matter, for example lead plates several centimetres to decimetres thick, but complete protection is almost impossible.

Gamma radiation is also used for technical applications, for example in sensors or nuclear power plants. However, sufficient radiation protection must always be ensured.

9.7. Half-life

A radioactive atom is unstable. This means that it decays and loses part of its mass.

In connection with radioactivity, the question often arises of how long a radioactive substance radiates. Some substances decay into stable atoms within just a few seconds and are thus no longer radioactive. Other substances, however, including those widely used in energy production, such as uranium or plutonium, radiate for centuries or even longer.

But how much time passes between a decay? It varies, the reason being that radioactive decay is a random event. As soon as the atom is unstable, there is a possibility of decay. When the decay actually occurs it is random. However, it can be observed that certain substances decay faster than others. Therefore, one can conclude that these tend to decay earlier.

In order to be able to make a statement about the "shelf life", the so-called **half-life** $T_{1/2}$ is introduced.

First we need to understand that radioactive decay is a random, exponential process. The more atoms that are left, the more decay.

The half-life of a potential decay indicates the **average time** after which the mass of the radioactive substance has **halved. In** other words, after a half-life $T_{1/2}$ half of all unstable atoms have decayed, the other half have not yet.

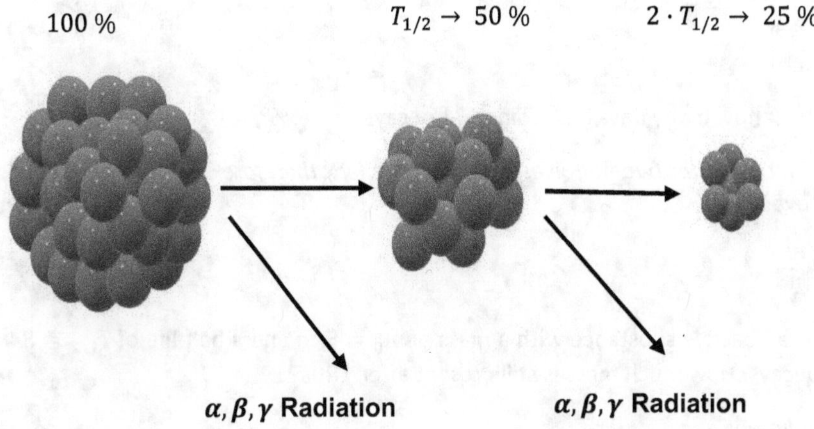

Figure 75: Representation of the half-life

After a further half-life, i.e. after a total of two half-lives $2 \cdot T_{1/2}$ only half of the half, i.e. 25%, has not yet decayed, and so on.

To calculate the mass after a given half-life, we get:

$$m(t) = m_0 \cdot \frac{1}{2^{\frac{t}{T_{1/2}}}}$$

$m(t)$: *Mass at time* t ; m_0: *initial mass* $(t = 0)$

From a radioactive mass of $m_0 = 500g$ after three half-lives $t = 3 \cdot T_{1/2}$ only
$m(3 \cdot T_{1/2}) = 500\ g \cdot \frac{1}{2^{\frac{3 \cdot T_{1/2}}{T_{1/2}}}} = 500g \cdot \frac{1}{2^3} = 62.5g$ remains.

The following table shows the half-lives of various radioactive substances.

Radioactive isotope	Half-life
Iodine 131	8 days
Cobalt 60	5.27 years
Plutonium 239	24110 years
Uranium 235	703,800,000 (700 million) years
Uranium 238	4,470,000,000 (4.4 billion) years

After how many days has iodine 131 decayed to 75%?

Solution: After two half-lives, only 25% are left, therefore 75% have already decayed.

A radioactive substance with a mass of $m_0 = 5kg$ and a half-life of $T_{1/2} = 34\ s$ decays. How much mass is still present after $180s$?

Solution:

$$m(180) = 5\ kg \cdot \frac{1}{2^{\frac{300s}{34\ s}}} = 11.04\ g$$

A substance decomposes after three days from $m_0 = 15\ t$ to $m(3\ d) = 5\ kg$.

What is the half-life of the substance?

Solution:

We insert the given values and solve for the half-life

$$m(3\ d) = 15000\ kg \cdot \frac{1}{2^{\frac{3\ d}{T_{1/2}}}} = 5\ kg$$

$$\frac{15000\ kg}{5\ kg} = 2^{\frac{3\ d}{T_{1/2}}}$$

Now we have to draw a logarithm. The logarithm of two is a good choice.

$$\frac{15000\ kg}{5\ kg} = 2^{\frac{3\ d}{T_{\frac{1}{2}}}} \rightarrow \log_2 \frac{15000\ kg}{5\ kg} = \frac{3\ d}{T_{\frac{1}{2}}}$$

$$T_{\frac{1}{2}} = \frac{3\ d}{\log_2 \frac{15000\ kg}{5\ kg}} = \frac{3\ d}{11.55} = 0.26\ d = 6.24\ h$$

The half-life is about 6.24 h.

This concludes the topic of atomic physics and radiation theory.

In the meantime, we also understand why nuclear power and the resulting nuclear waste is harmful and why long-term storage facilities are being discussed. Uranium, which we use today for our electricity generation, will continue to emit harmful radiation for several billion years.

This brings us almost to the end of the panoramic view through the multifaceted subject areas of physics.

Almost, because there is still one chapter left that was shaped by one, if not the most famous physicist. We are talking, of course, about Albert Einstein and the theory of relativity.

10. Theory of relativity

The theory of relativity is a very young theory. It investigates the relationship between time, space and gravity. We all know the founder of the theory of relativity. What is less well known is that the physicists Hendrik Lorentz and Henri Poincaré did considerable preliminary work on which Einstein built.

The theory of relativity is divided into the **special theory of special relativity** which was published in 1905 and the **general theory of general relativity** which was added in 1916.

The special theory of relativity forms the basis, which is easier to understand and which we will look at in more detail. The general theory of rel-

Figure 76: Albert Einstein in his younger years

ativity builds on this and adds other aspects, especially the influence of gravity.

As the name suggests, the theory of relativity describes that all physical relationships must be viewed as relative to each other.

Moreover, the entire world view is turned upside down. Objects moving at almost the speed of light suddenly become shorter and time is not rigid but can stretch like a rubber rope.

10.1. Relativity and inertial systems

A term coined by Einstein is that of **inertial systems** or **inertial reference frames.**

An inertial reference frame describes a **closed system** in which all objects behave according to **Newton's laws.** A body at rest will remain at rest, a body moving uniformly will remain in motion.

Accelerated systems, on the other hand, do not form inertial systems. These include, for example, rotating systems. An accelerating car also does not constitute an inertial system.

An inertial reference frame is not accelerated or spinning. Inertial systems always move relative to each other.

To understand what is meant by relativity in the first place, let's look at a journey in an ICE train. The train forms a closed inertial reference frame that moves **relative to** the rest of the world at a constant rate $v = 300 \; \frac{km}{h}$. A passenger on the train does not even notice that he is currently moving with $v = 300 \; \frac{km}{h}$ moving. For him, he himself is not in motion within the inertial system, his speed is therefore $v = 0 \; \frac{km}{h}$. Only when he looks out of the window can he realise that he is moving relative to the outer inertial system, or that the outer inertial system is moving relative to him.

This is exactly what the principle of relativity says. All inertial reference frames always move at a **relative speed** to each other. The train moves with $v = 300 \; \frac{km}{h}$ relative to the external observer!

However, there is a constant in the universe. Let's imagine again that we are standing in a long aisle of the moving train. We switch on a laser pointer and shine it along the aisle. The light spreads out with the speed of light of $c = 300 \cdot 10^8 \; \frac{km}{h}$. But what does this experiment look like to an outside observer?

According to the current state of knowledge, the speed of the train and that of the light must add up. The light therefore propagates with $v_{light} = v_{train} + c$.

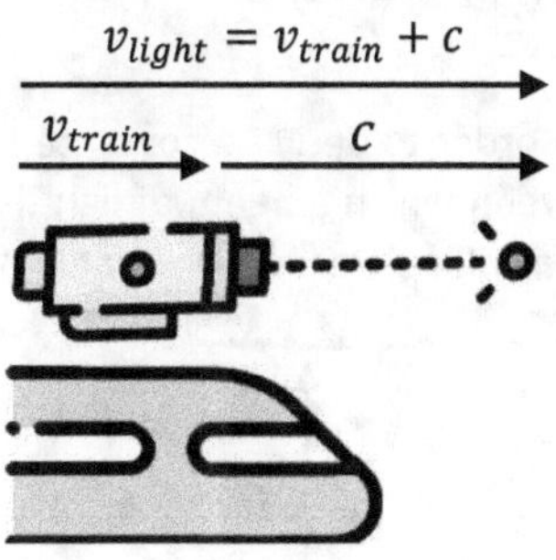

Figure 77: Laser pointer and train speeds add up (not!)

Measurements showed, however, that the speed still corresponds to the speed of light, i.e. $v_{light} = c$.

This phenomenon is one of the fundamental pillars of special and general relativity. The speed of light is the fastest possible speed in any inertial frame. It is invariable, which is why we speak of the **constancy of the speed of light**.

The only solution to the problem described, where the speed of light can be measured both times, is that **time or space** behaves differently in the two systems. For the speed is merely distance per time, $v = \frac{s}{t}$.

If the speed remains the same, space must shorten or time must increase.

This realisation, the **relativity of time and space,** leads to the first revolutionary aspect of relativity - **time dilation**.

10.2. Time dilation

 Time dilation describes that time passes more slowly in a moving inertial system than in a stationary one.

For the occupants of the moving inertial system, time does not pass faster or slower, but "normally fast".

 Within the inertial system, they do not perceive themselves as moving. Instead, for the occupants, the other inertial frame is moving relative to theirs (remember, everything is always relative to one another). Therefore, they also perceive the time of the other inertial frame as being slower.

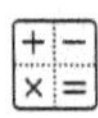

In order to derive a concrete formula, we use two mirrors at a distance of l between which a beam of light is reflected back and forth. For the sake of clarity, we will only consider a single photon, not the entire light beam.

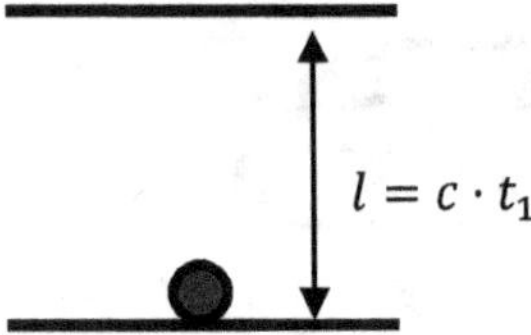

Figure 78: A photon is reflected by two mirrors

When the photon is reflected once, it has covered a total distance of

$$s = l = c \cdot t_1.$$

Next, we look at what happens when both mirrors move constantly in one direction. The inertial frame of the mirrors does not change at all. Just like the experiment with the train, you can't notice that they are moving.

From the outside, however, the photon has travelled along a different path. Namely, a diagonal.

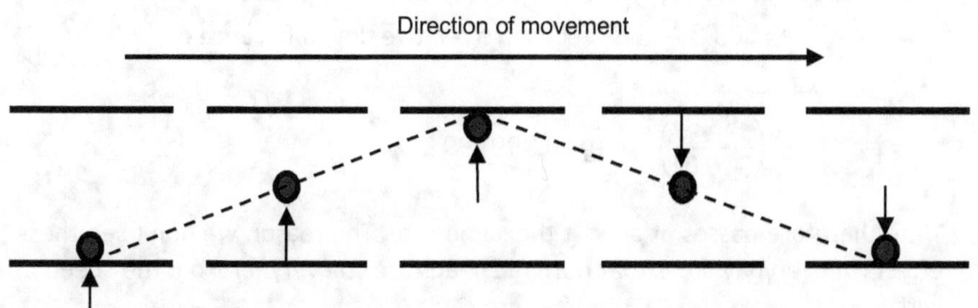

Figure 79: Travelled path of the photon from the observer's point of view

We can calculate the distance covered with the Pythagorean theorem.

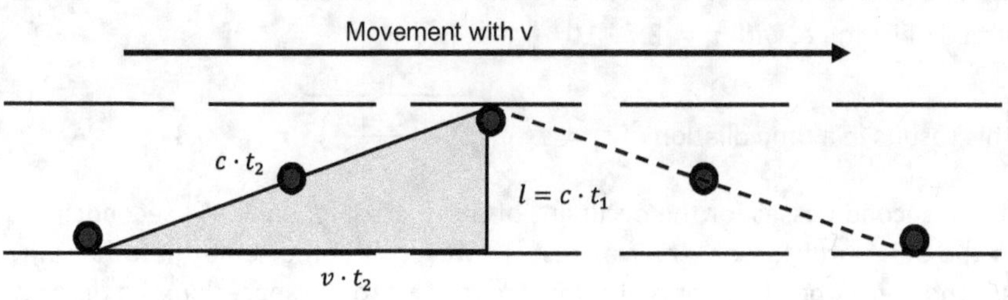

Figure 80: Calculation of the time difference

$$(c \cdot t_2)^2 = (v \cdot t_2)^2 + (c \cdot t_1)^2$$

$$c^2 \cdot t_2^2 = v^2 \cdot t_2^2 + c^2 \cdot t_1^2$$

$$t_1^2 = t_2^2 \cdot \frac{c^2 - v^2}{c^2}$$

Finally, if we solve for the time t_1 we get a concrete formula with which we can calculate the time difference. We need the velocity difference v and the speed of light c. The time t_1 which has elapsed in the system at rest compared to the elapsed time t_2 in the moving system results from:

$$t_1 = t_2 \cdot \sqrt{1 - \left(\frac{v}{c}\right)^2}$$

For the speed of the train, which moves relative to the station with a speed of $v = 300 \, \frac{km}{h} = 83.8 \, \frac{m}{s}$ this results in a relative time difference of:

$$t_1 = t_2 \cdot \sqrt{1 - \left(\frac{83.8}{3 \cdot 10^8}\right)^2} = t_B \cdot 0.999999 \ldots$$

Time therefore passes at almost the same rate. The reason we don't see these effects in everyday life is that normal speeds are still very far from the speed of light.

This makes time dilation so marginal that we cannot perceive it.

These effects become noticeable when we approach the speed of light. Let us assume that we manage to build a spaceship that can move us at 90 % of the speed of light, i.e. with $v = 2.7 \cdot 10^8 \, \frac{m}{s}$ that is.

This results in a time dilation of $t_1 = t_2 \cdot \sqrt{1 - \left(\frac{2.7 \cdot 10^8}{3 \cdot 10^8}\right)^2} = t_B \cdot 0.44$

If one second passes for the occupant of the spaceship, only 0.44 seconds pass in the system of the observer at rest. However, it is the same the other way around. Since the observer is also moving relative to the spaceship, the time for the occupant of the spaceship is reduced from one second on Earth to only 0.44 seconds.

We can already accelerate individual atoms to almost the speed of light, but so far we are still very far away from speeds at which time dilation exerts a noticeable influence for larger objects.

However, if we imagine that it is possible, we come to paradoxical experiments, for example the twin paradox, which Einstein himself presented in 1911.

10.3. The twin paradox:

Twins are born. We name the twins Max and Moritz.

Max flies with the help of a spaceship at a speed of $\vec{v} = 0.9 \cdot c$ to another star. Moritz remains behind on Earth.

Seen from Earth, time passes more slowly in Max's spaceship. When Max comes back to Earth after 30 Earth years, the only time that has passed for him is

$$t_{Max} = t_{Moritz} \cdot \sqrt{1 - \left(\frac{0.9 \cdot c}{c}\right)^2} = 30 \, a \cdot \sqrt{1 - (0.9)^2} = 30 \, a \cdot 0.44 = 13 \, a.$$

While Moritz has aged 30 years, his brother Max has only aged 13 years.

This is a nice mind game that violates some assumptions of time dilation. What could they be?

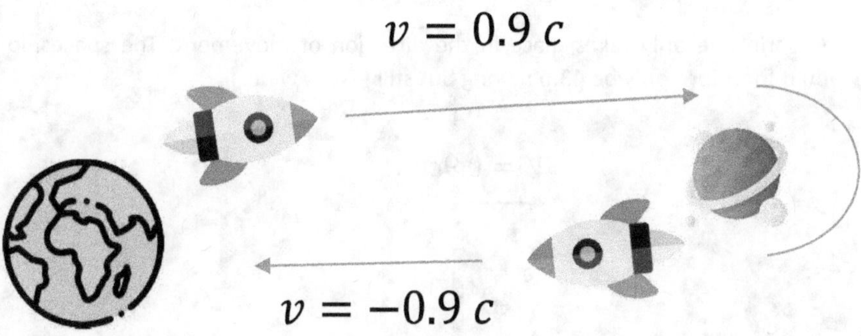

Figure 81: Twin paradox

Many factors violate the assumption that the spaceship and the Earth are one inertial system. The spaceship must first be accelerated to 90 % of the speed of light. In addition, the spaceship must turn around to get back to Earth. In the process, it is braked and accelerated.

The essential point, however, is that the speed on the return flight is no longer, $\vec{v} = 0.9 \cdot c$ but $\vec{v} = -0.9 \cdot c$ is. This is because the speed always has a magnitude and a direction.

10.4. Length contraction

We have established that we cannot rigidly separate time and space in moving inertial frames. The two physical quantities are closely interrelated and are combined to form so-called **space-time.** That is why an analogous effect appears alongside time dilation, the **length contraction** or also called **Lorentz contraction.**

If the speed of light is constant, time can change in different systems or the length of the object can shorten.

In length contraction, the space of a moving object shortens in the direction of the movement by the factor $\sqrt{1 - \left(\frac{v}{c}\right)^2}$

A spaceship which is $L_0 = 100\ m$ long and moving at 90 % of the speed of light, shrinks to the length for the observer:

$$L_0 = L \cdot \sqrt{1 - \left(\frac{v}{c}\right)^2} = 100\ m \cdot \sqrt{1 - (0.9)^2} = 43.6\ m$$

The shrinkage only takes place in the direction of movement. The spaceship would therefore only be 43.6 m long but still just as wide.

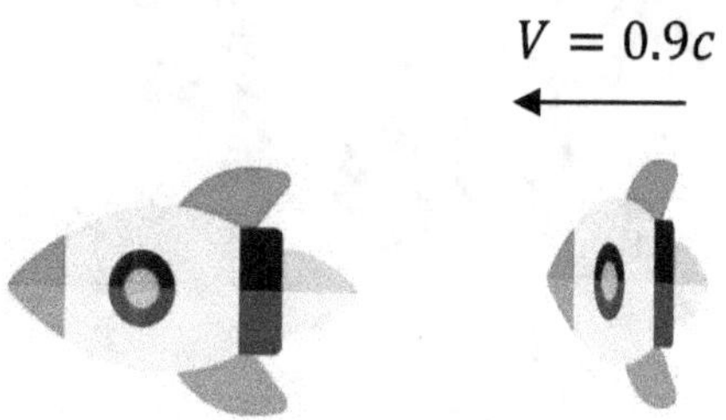

Figure 82: Length contraction in the direction of movement

10.5. Newton's simplification in everyday life

We have covered the effects of time dilation and length contraction but does that mean that all the previous chapters are wrong? Was Newton talking non-sense? The answer is yes and no.

> The trick is that the speed of light is so incredibly fast compared to our everyday speeds.

As an example we take the formulas for the momentum $p = m \cdot v$

This formula is approximately correct if we apply it to our everyday velocities. The correct formula for momentum would be

$$p = \frac{m \cdot v}{\sqrt{1 - \left(\frac{v}{c}\right)^2}}$$

Even if a rocket travels through space at $v = 1000\ \frac{km}{h} = 278\ \frac{m}{s}$, that is still only 0.000093% of the speed of light. Therefore, the prefactors such as $\frac{1}{\sqrt{1 - \left(\frac{v}{c}\right)^2}}$ which Einstein added, are negligible.

This concludes our journey through physics. Of course, it is not necessary for the complete content of the book to be understood immediately and that every formula should be learnt off by heart. That shows neither diligence nor intelligence. Even Einstein knew:

"Learning is experience. Everything else is simply information".

-Albert Einstein

Practice makes perfect, there are countless other facets of physics that help us to understand our world better, bit by bit.

Thank you for buying this book. Since the printing of the book is done directly by Amazon and I have no influence on the quality of the images, it is possible that some details may be lost.

That is why I offer the eBook in colour for free as a PDF file when you buy the book. There, all the pictures are in high resolution and you always get the latest version.

To do so, send a message with the subject "Physics eBook EN", as well as a screenshot of the purchase or proof of the order at Amazon to the email:

Benjamin-Spahic@web.de

I will send you the eBook immediately.

If you miss something, don't like it or have suggestions for improvement or questions, feel free to send me an email.

Constructive criticism is important in order to be able to improve something. I am constantly revising the book and am happy to respond to any constructive suggestions for improvement.

Otherwise, if you liked the book, I would also appreciate a positive review on Amazon. That helps to increase the visibility of the book and is the greatest praise an author can receive.

Yours, Benjamin

Disclaimer

The author assumes no responsibility for the topicality, completeness and correctness of the information provided. Furthermore, no guarantee can be given for the achievement of the described skills.